D1637458

Data Processing Manager's Model Reports and Formats

Ralph L. Kliem
Irwin S. Ludin

PRENTICE HALL
Englewood Cliffs, New Jersey 07632

Prentice-Hall International (UK) Limited, *London*
Prentice-Hall of Australia Pty. Limited, *Sydney*
Prentice-Hall Canada, Inc., *Toronto*
Prentice-Hall Hispanoamericana, S.A., *Mexico*
Prentice-Hall of India Private Limited, *New Delhi*
Prentice-Hall of Japan, Inc., *Tokyo*
Simon & Schuster Asia Pte. Ltd., *Singapore*
Editora Prentice-Hall do Brasil, Ltda., *Rio de Janeiro*

© 1992 *by*

Prentice Hall, Inc.

Englewood Cliffs, New Jersey

10 9 8 7 6 5 4 3 2

Library of Congress Cataloging-in-Publication Data

Kliem, Ralph L.
    Data processing manager's model reports and formats / by Ralph L.
Kliem and Irwin S. Ludin.
      p. cm.
    Includes bibliographical references and index.
    ISBN 0-13-203068-3
    1. Electronic data processing documentation. I. Ludin, Irwin S.
II. Title.
QA76.9.D6K58 1991
005.1'5—dc20   91-26956
                                               CIP

ISBN 0-13-203068-3

PRENTICE HALL
Business Information & Publishing Division
Englewood Cliffs, NJ 07632
Simon & Schuster, A Paramount Communications Company

Printed in the United States of America

For my wife, Janet, and my children, Melissa and Michael
Irwin S. Ludin

For my wife, Priscilla, and my daughter, Tonia
Ralph L. Kliem

PREFACE

Data Processing Manager's Model Reports and Formats is your key to success for:

- Saving time. No longer do you have to start from scratch trying to figure out the content or logic of a report, plan, chart, or form. Wonder what goes into a requirements study document? You can find the answer in this book.

- Reducing effort. You won't have to conduct extensive research on what goes into a report, plan, chart, form, or diagram because you'll have this book to help you get started. Just use the outlines as a guide, or copy or modify any forms for your use.

- Increasing productivity. If you manage people, you can have them use the book as a reference to find the contents of a report, plan, chart, form, or specific diagram. They can then concentrate on other matters by not having to "re-invent the wheel." If you're a consultant, you can concentrate on the critical issues rather than spend crucial time trying to determine the contents of a particular document or diagram.

- Saving money. The book covers a wide spectrum of reports, plans, diagrams, charts, logs, and checklists used during the software life cycle. You can decrease reliance on expensive consultants or additional staff by using this book.

- Providing standardization. If reports, plans, diagrams, charts, logs, and checklists with varying formats and contents have made communications within your organization difficult, this book can provide the consistency that you need.

This book is an essential tool for any data processing organization that wants to function cost-effectively. Without it, you may be allowing your business practices to eat away at your company's major reason for its existence—profits.

INTRODUCTION

One of the great ironies of the field of data processing is that the field requires much documentation to develop a paperless system or to run a computing organization. The standards for the format and content of that documentation varies widely from company to company. That often leads to communication problems among computing professionals.

Although this book will not eliminate such communication problems, it offers a step in the right direction. It is full of checklists, outlines, forms, and diagrams that you can reference, review, modify, or copy whenever necessary.

The book offers other advantages, too. It provides a basis for building more elaborate reports, helps standardize documentation within your organization, and stops the "re-inventing the wheel" syndrome because everyone can reference it whenever necessary rather than start from scratch.

The book is divided into four sections.

Section I, "Development," provides documentation created during each phase of the software development life cycle. For instance, you will see an outline of a feasibility study for the Feasibility Study phase of a development project.

Section II, "Sustaining," provides documentation created or referenced once a system has been implemented in the user's environment. This section presents documentation related to maintenance and enhancements to an existing system.

Section III, "Operations," provides documentation referenced or completed during the daily activities of a data processing organization. This section presents documentation related to data center operations, security, users, and training.

Section IV, "Administrative," covers support documentation referenced or created throughout the development, sustaining, and operations activities that occur within a typical data processing department. It presents documentation related to configuration management, quality, standards, project/program management, data center management, and subcontractor management.

Each type of documentation has an overview page that describes it. The overview page gives the description, objectives, organization, and schedule for use for that specific document.

The organization subsection of the overview page lists the positions in a typical data processing department having some use for the documentation. These positions, having a unique numeric designation, can then be referenced in the Organization and Responsibilities Chart in this chapter. The reader can then obtain an overall understanding of who needs what documentation and to what extent, such as to prepare, review, or update it. For example, you can find the extent of responsibilities of the Manager of Development (1.0) and the Steering Committee (2.0) listed in the organization subsection in the Feasibility Study Document Overview, in the Organization and Responsibilities Chart. You do that by using their unique numbers (1.0) and (2.0) in the organization subsection of the overview and locating those same numbers in the chart.

The schedule subsection of the overview page lists when the documentation would be useful and to what extent, such as review or update, to data processing professionals. Each phase listed, having a unique numeric designation, can be referenced in the Software Life Cycle Chart in this chapter. The reader can then obtain an overall understanding of when certain documentation is needed and to what extent, such as reviewed or updated. For example, you can find the extent that the Feasibility Study is used during which phases by reviewing the schedule subsection in the Feasibility Study Overview. Then, using the unique designator for each phase, reference those phases in the Software Life Cycle Chart. You can do that by locating the phase with its unique numeric designator, which in this case is 1.0, the Feasibility phase.

At the conclusion of the book, you will find a glossary. You can reference it to determine the documentation that you need. Having read the applicable definitions, you can then turn to the applicable overview page for further information.

This book presents documentation from the perspective of the data processing department. Keep in mind, however, that department alone cannot develop or complete the great magnitude of documentation with the participation of many other organizations throughout a company. Procurement, purchasing, legal, finance, and others play a crucial role in developing or completing some of the documentation. Remember, too, one other party who has a crucial role in the current and future activities of a data processing organization: the users. Indeed, their input and feedback is essential for developing and maintaining accurate and complete data processing documentation.

HOW TO USE THIS BOOK

Data Processing Manager's Model Reports and Formats is divided into four sections. Each one presents outlines, checklists, logs, charts, and examples of diagrams that you can copy, modify, or use for reference.

Section I, "Development," provides outlines for studies, plans, and reports developed during each phase of the software development life cycle. You will see, for example, outlines for the feasibility study, requirements definition, functional specifications, and detail design documents. In addition, this section gives you checklists, forms, and diagrams covering a wide range of technical subjects, like data modeling, data dictionary, process specifications, prototyping, software ergonomics, record layouts, file descriptions, structure charts, flowcharts, and decision tables.

Section II, "Sustaining," presents outlines for reports as well as checklists and diagrams pertaining to maintenance and enhancements to an existing system. For example, you'll find for your use a programming checklist and a system upgrade checklist.

Section III, "Operations," presents outlines for plans, procedures, guides, and manuals, as well as logs and checklists covering four important areas: data center operations, security, documentation, and training. For example, you'll see outlines for data center, audit, and training plans.

Section IV, "Administrative," gives you outlines for plans, procedures, guides, and manuals, as well as forms and checklists covering six key areas: configuration management, quality, standards, project/program management, data center administration, and subcontractor management. You'll discover outlines for a configuration management plan, software quality-assurance plan, and standards and guidelines manual. You'll also find examples of work breakdown structures, resource histograms, and network diagrams. Finally, you'll see checklists on risk assessment, directives, runbooks, and performance validation.

Each outline, form, checklist, log, and diagram within a section has an overview page that describes it. The overview page gives a description, objectives, organization, and schedule.

The organization section of the overview page lists the positions in a typical data processing department for which a particular item in this book would be useful. You can refer to these positions in the Organization and Responsibilities Chart to determine exactly which tasks each one performs.

The schedule section of the overview page lists the phases in which a document is used. By referring to the Software Life Cycle Chart you can determine these phases.

The following example of a payroll system will show you how to use this book. Let's start with development of the payroll system.

Since you're starting to develop the system, you'll need a statement of work defining your charter and the necessary deliverables. Turning to Section I, you'll see an outline of a statement of work (Chapter 1). Then, having the statement of work completed and approved, you'll proceed through the rest of the software development life cycle by copying, modifying, or referencing items like data models (Chapter 2); alternatives analysis document (Chapter 3); functional specifications document (Chapter 4); system design (Chapter 5); code and test plans and reports (Chapter 6); verification/validation plan (Chapter 7); system conversion plan (Chapter 9); and installation and implementation plan (Chapter 10). As you can see, you'll have access to a "straw horse" to relieve you of the stress of "re-inventing the wheel" when developing a new system.

Once you have completed development, you can proceed to Section II. The payroll system is sustained by changing it periodically. If you modify the system, you can refer to the chapter on maintenance (Chapter 11) or enhancements (Chapter 12). However, you might go back through Section I and review, for instance, the feasibility study and cost–benefit analysis documents (Chapter 1) to determine whether to modify them.

As development and sustaining activities occur, you can refer to Section III for forms, checklists, and other documents regarding management of the system on an ongoing basis, including in a data center. You might want to develop material on protecting the data center that will house the payroll system and the payroll system itself by referring to the chapter on security (Chapter 14). Since the payroll system is new, you'll want to develop user documentation (Chapter 15) to facilitate its usage as well as build a training plan and student handouts (Chapter 16) for training staff in the use of the system.

During development, sustaining, or operations, you'll perform a wide range of administrative functions. You can refer to Section IV to help you. You'll need to develop a configuration management plan (Chapter 17) and address areas related to quality (Chapter 18). You may also need to develop a disaster recovery plan (Chapter 19) for the data center that runs the payroll system.

During the development of the payroll system, you'll need to plan, organize, and control your project using project management tools (Chapter 20) like work breakdown structures and schedules.

This assistance in four major areas of data processing—development, sustaining, operations, and administration—means that you'll no longer need to re-invent the wheel. Instead, you'll be able to minimize your oversights and maximize your rewards. So sit back and relax.

CONTENTS

Section IV   Administrative   255

ORGANIZATION AND RESPONSIBILITIES CHART

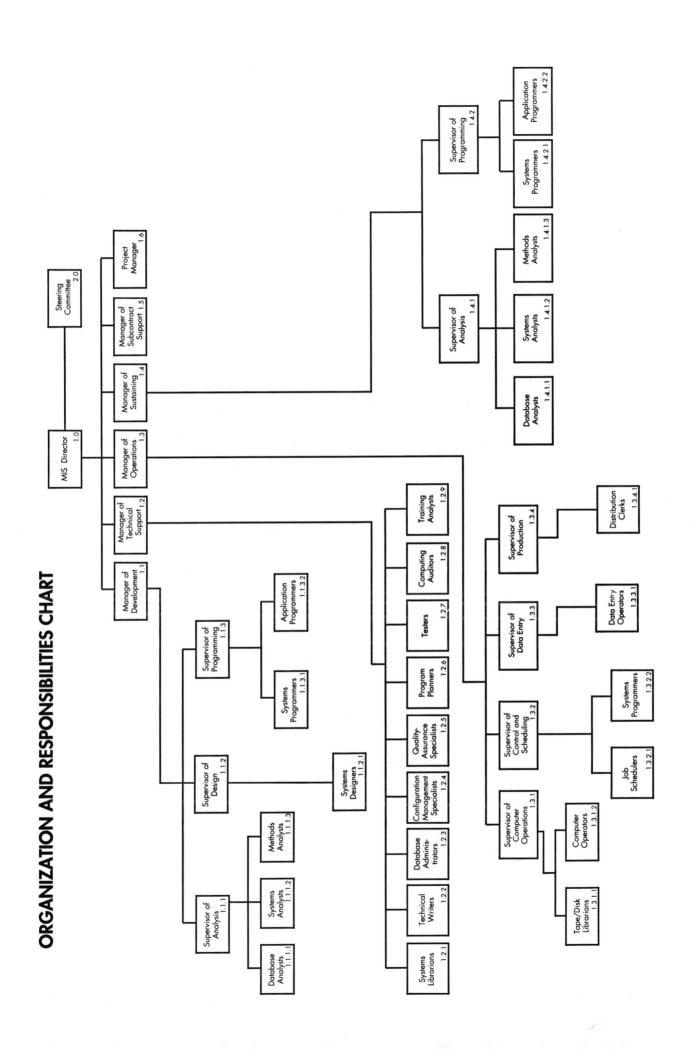

ORGANIZATION AND RESPONSIBILITIES CHART

1.0 MIS DIRECTOR

- Reviews Data Center—Operations Plan
- Reviews Audit Plan
- Reviews Training Plan
- Reviews Project Plan
- Prepares Organization Chart

1.1 MANAGER OF DEVELOPMENT

- Reviews and approves Database Specifications Document
- Reviews and approves System Conversion Plan
- Reviews Audit Plan
- Reviews and approves Configuration Management Plan
- Prepares Organization Charts
- Reviews and approves Feasibility Study Document
- Reviews and approves Statement of Work

1.1.1 SUPERVISOR OF ANALYSIS

- Reviews System/Subsystem Specifications Checklist
- Reviews and approves Database Specifications Document
- Reviews and approves System Conversion Plan
- Prepares Installation and Implementation Plan
- Reviews Audit Plan
- Generates Statistical Quality-Control Graphs
- Reviews Statement of Work
- Completes Statistical Quality-Control Checklist
- Prepares Organization Charts

1.1.1.1 DATABASE ANALYSTS

- Refer to Data Dictionary
- Develop Entity Relationship Diagram
- Prepare Database Specifications Document

- Refer to Record Layout Form
- Prepare Logical Database Structure
- Prepare Data Models
- Prepare Functional Specifications Document
- Prepare Database Design Flowcharts

1.1.1.2 SYSTEMS ANALYSTS

- Prepare Cost–Benefit Analysis Document
- Build Data Dictionary
- Develop Entity Relationship Diagram
- Use Structured English
- Develop and update Data-Flow Diagrams
- Develop Process Specification
- Complete Prototyping Checklist
- Prepare Requirements Definition Document
- Prepare Alternatives Analysis Document
- Prepare and complete Record Layout Form
- Complete File Description Form
- Complete Software Ergonomics Checklist
- Prepare Detail Design Document
- Develop Decision Table
- Develop Decision Tree
- Prepare Data Models
- Prepare Functional Specification Document
- Develop Test Plan
- Refer to Verification/Validation Test Checklist
- Prepare User Manual
- Prepare Desk Procedures
- Prepare Computer Operator Manual
- Prepare Standards and Guidelines Manual
- Prepare Disaster Recovery Plan
- Complete Software Documentation Checklist
- Prepare System Flowchart
- Complete Report Layout Form

1.1.1.3 METHODS ANALYSTS

- Prepare User Manual
- Prepare Desk Procedures
- Prepare Computer Operator Manual
- Refer to Statistical Quality-Control Graphs
- Refer to Statistical Quality-Control Checklist
- Prepare Standards and Guidelines Manual
- Prepare Disaster Recovery Plan
- Complete Software Documentation Checklist
- Prepare Cost–Benefit Analysis Document

1.1.2 SUPERVISOR OF DESIGN

- Reviews Audit Plan
- Prepares Organization Chart
- Reviews Statement of Work

1.1.2.1 SYSTEMS DESIGNERS

- Refer to Data Dictionary
- Refer to Entity Relationship Diagram
- Use Structured English
- Refer to Data-Flow Diagrams
- Refer to Process Specification
- Prepare and update System/Subsystem Specifications Checklist
- Prepare Functional Specifications Document
- Develop Structure Charts
- Prepare Preliminary Design Document
- Review Decision Table
- Review Decision Tree

1.1.3 SUPERVISOR OF PROGRAMMING

- Reviews and approves Verification/Validation Plan
- Reviews System Conversion Plan
- Reviews System Conversion Checklist
- Reviews Programming Checklist
- Reviews Data Center—Operations Plan

- Reviews Audit Plan
- Approves Software Version Form
- Reviews Patch Request Form
- Prepares Organization Chart
- Reviews Statement of Work

1.1.3.1 SYSTEMS PROGRAMMERS

- Refer to Data Dictionary
- Refer to Data-Flow Diagrams
- Refer to Process Specification
- Review Record Layout Form
- Complete File Description Form
- Review Structure Chart
- Develop Nassi–Shneiderman Charts
- Develop Program Flowchart
- Develop System Flowchart
- Prepare Detail Design Document
- Develop and review Decision Table
- Develop and review Decision Tree
- Review Verification/Validation Plan
- Refer to Verification/Validation Test Checklist
- Refer to System Conversion Plan
- Refer to System Conversion Checklist
- Refer to Installation and Implementation Package Form
- Refer to Installation and Implementation Checklist
- Refer to Programming Checklist
- Approve Software Version Form
- Complete Patch Request Form
- Prepare Runbook Checklist

1.1.3.2 APPLICATION PROGRAMMERS

- Refer to Data Dictionary
- Refer to Data-Flow Diagrams
- Refer to Process Specification
- Review Record Layout Form
- Complete File Description Form

- Review Structure Chart
- Develop Nassi–Shneiderman Charts
- Develop Program Flowchart
- Develop System Flowchart
- Review Report Layout Form
- Prepare Detail Design Document
- Develop and review Decision Table
- Develop and review Decision Tree
- Refer to Test Report Form
- Develop Hierarchy Input–Process–Output (HIPO) Documentation
- Review Verification/Validation Plan
- Refer to Verification/Validation Test Checklist
- Refer to System Conversion Plan
- Refer to System Conversion Checklist
- Refer to Installation and Implementation Package Form
- Refer to Installation and Implementation Checklist
- Refer to Programming Checklist
- Approve Software Version Form
- Complete Patch Request Form
- Prepare Runbook Checklist

1.2 MANAGER OF TECHNICAL SUPPORT

- Reviews and approves Database Specifications Document
- Reviews and approves Verification/Validation Plan
- Reviews and approves System Conversion Plan
- Reviews and approves Data Conversion Plan
- Reviews and approves Data Center—Operations Plan
- Reviews Audit Plan
- Reviews and approves Configuration Management Plan
- Approves Software Version Form
- Reviews Configuration Audit Checklist
- Reviews and approves Software Quality Assurance Plan
- Prepares Organization Charts
- Reviews Performance Validation Checklist

1.2.1 SYSTEMS LIBRARIANS

- Refer to Data Conversion Checklist
- Maintain Installation and Implementation Package Form
- Maintain System Utilization Log Form
- Maintain Machine-Run Log Form
- Maintain System Incidence Log Form
- Refer to Software Program Requirement Log Form
- Refer to Software Program Distribution Form
- Maintain Runbook Checklist
- Maintain Data Models

1.2.2 TECHNICAL WRITERS

- Prepare and update User Manual
- Prepare and update Desk Procedures
- Prepare and update Computer Operator Manual
- Prepare and update Standards and Guidelines Manual
- Complete Software Documentation Checklist

1.2.3 DATABASE ADMINISTRATORS

- Maintain Data Dictionary
- Maintain Database Design Flowcharts
- Review Database Specifications Document
- Review and approve Data Conversion Plan
- Review Data Conversion Checklist

1.2.4 CONFIGURATION MANAGEMENT SPECIALISTS

- Refer to Data Models
- Refer to Data-Flow Diagrams
- Refer to Requirements Definition Document
- Refer to Alternatives Analysis Document
- Refer to Functional Specifications Document
- Refer to Database Specification Document
- Refer to Structure Chart Checklist
- Refer to Database Design Flowcharts
- Refer to Preliminary Design Document

- Refer to Detail Design Document
- Develop and refer to Test Plan
- Refer to Verification/Validation Plan
- Review System Conversion Plan
- Review Data Conversion Plan
- Review Installation and Implementation Plan
- Review System Upgrade Checklist
- Refer to Data Center—Operations Plan
- Prepare Configuration Management Plan
- Complete and maintain Software Version Form
- Maintain Problem Report Form and Flowchart
- Complete and maintain Configuration Audit Checklist
- Refer to File Archive Form
- Maintain Patch Request Form
- Refer to Software Quality-Assurance Plan
- Prepare and maintain Maintenance Control Report Form
- Refer to Project Plan
- Refer to Bar (Gantt) Chart
- Refer to Network Diagrams
- Refer to Work Breakdown Structure
- Refer to Project Schedule Report Form
- Complete and maintain Manual-Checkout Form
- Review Performance Validation Checklist

1.2.5 QUALITY-ASSURANCE SPECIALISTS

- Develop Test Plan
- Review and approve Verification/Validation Plan
- Review and approve Verification/Validation Test Checklist
- Review Subsystem Test Report Form
- Review System Test Report Form
- Review System Conversion Plan
- Refer to Data Center—Operations Plan
- Approve Software Version Form
- Review Configuration Audit Checklist
- Prepare Software Quality-Assurance Plan
- Refer to Maintenance Control Report Form
- Complete Performance Validation Checklist

1.2.6 PROGRAM PLANNERS

- Generate System Performance Graphs
- Generate System Productivity Graphs
- Prepare Bar (Gantt) Chart
- Generate Activity Relationship Report Form
- Develop Network Diagrams
- Develop Work Breakdown Structure
- Generate Resource Histogram
- Complete Status Update Form
- Generate Resource Usage Report Form
- Complete Resource Usage Form
- Generate Project Schedule Report Form
- Prepare Monthly Status Report Form
- Generate Project Cost Report Form
- Generate ''S'' Cost Curve
- Prepare Directives Checklist

1.2.7 TESTERS

- Review Process Specifications
- Review Software Ergonomics Checklist
- Develop Test Plan
- Develop, complete, and maintain Test Report Form
- Develop Verification/Validation Plan
- Develop, complete, and maintain Verification/Validation Test Completion Report Form
- Complete Verification/Validation Test Checklist
- Complete Subsystem Test Report Form
- Complete System Test Report Form
- Review System Conversion Plan
- Complete Installation and Implementation Package Form
- Complete Installation and Implementation Test Checklist
- Refer to Data Center—Operations Plan
- Approve Software Version Form
- Approve Problem Report Form and Flowchart
- Review Configuration Audit Checklist
- Refer to Software Quality-Assurance Plan

• Complete Performance Validation Checklist

1.2.8 COMPUTING AUDITORS

• Prepare Audit Plan
• Complete Computing Facility Controls Checklist
• Complete System Access Controls Checklist
• Refer to Configuration Audit Checklist
• Refer to Software Quality-Assurance Plan
• Complete Risk Assessment Checklist
• Refer to Performance Validation Checklist

1.2.9 TRAINING ANALYSTS

• Prepare Training Plan
• Prepare Instructor's Guide
• Prepare Student Handout
• Prepare Training Schedule Form

1.3 MANAGER OF OPERATIONS

• Reviews and approves System Upgrade Checklist
• Reviews System Performance Graphs
• Reviews System Productivity Graphs
• Reviews and approves Data Center—Operations Plan
• Reviews Audit Plan
• Reviews Statistical Quality-Control Graphs
• Prepares Organization Charts

1.3.1 SUPERVISOR OF COMPUTER OPERATIONS

• Prepares Facility Usage Checklist
• Completes Equipment Maintenance Report Form
• Completes System Upgrade Checklist
• Reviews System Performance Graphs
• Reviews System Productivity Graphs
• Prepares Data Center—Operations Plan
• Completes Data Center—Operations Checklist
• Prepares Organization Charts

• Reviews Audit Plan

1.3.1.1 TAPE/DISK LIBRARIANS

• Maintain Software Program Requirement Log Form
• Complete and maintain Software Program Distribution Form
• Complete and maintain File Archive Form
• Complete and maintain File Request Form
• Complete and maintain Tape-Reel Archive Form
• Complete and maintain Scratch-Tape Reuse Form

1.3.1.2 COMPUTER OPERATORS

• Complete System Utilization Log Form
• Complete Machine-Run Log Form
• Complete System Incidence Log Form
• Complete Software Program Requirement Log Form
• Refer to Software Program Distribution Sheet Form
• Refer to Computer Operator Manual

1.3.2 SUPERVISOR OF CONTROL AND SCHEDULING

• Prepares Organization Charts

1.3.2.1 JOB SCHEDULERS

• Refer to System Flowchart
• Refer to Installation and Implementation Package Form
• Refer to System Utilization Log Form
• Refer to Machine-Run Log Form
• Refer to System Incidence Log Form
• Refer to Software Program Requirement Log
• Refer to Runbook Checklist

1.3.2.2 SYSTEMS PROGRAMMERS

• Review File Description Form
• Review Nassi–Shneiderman Charts
• Review Program Flowchart

- Review Systems Flowchart
- Refer to Software Version Form
- Refer to Patch Request Form
- Review Runbook Checklist

1.3.3 SUPERVISOR OF DATA ENTRY

- Prepares Organization Charts

1.3.3.1 DATA ENTRY OPERATORS

- Refer to User Manual
- Refer to Computer Operator Manual

1.3.4 SUPERVISOR OF PRODUCTION

- Prepares Organization Charts

1.3.4.1 DISTRIBUTION CLERKS

- Refer to Software Program Distribution Form
- Refer to Desk Procedures
- Refer to Manual-Checkout Form

1.4 MANAGER OF SUSTAINING

- Reviews and approves System Conversion Plan
- Reviews and approves Data Conversion Plan
- Reviews and approves Installation and Implementation Plan
- Reviews and approves System Upgrade Checklist
- Reviews System Performance Graphs
- Reviews System Productivity Graphs
- Prepares Data Center—Operations Plan
- Approves Software Quality-Assurance Plan
- Reviews Statistical Quality-Control Graphs
- Prepares Organization Charts

1.4.1 SUPERVISOR OF ANALYSIS

- Reviews Database Specifications Document
- Develops System Conversion Plan
- Reviews System Conversion Checklist
- Develops Data Conversion Plan
- Reviews Data Conversion Checklist
- Prepares Installation and Implementation Plan
- Reviews Installation and Implementation Test Checklist
- Completes System Upgrade Checklist
- Reviews Equipment Maintenance Report Form
- Generates Statistical Quality-Control Graphs
- Completes Statistical Quality-Control Checklist
- Prepares Organization Charts

1.4.1.1 DATABASE ANALYSTS

- Maintain Database Design Flowcharts
- Review Database Specifications Document
- Review Data Conversion Plan
- Review Data Conversion Checklist
- Approve Software Version Form
- Refer to Maintenance Control Report Form

1.4.1.2 SYSTEMS ANALYSTS

- Update Requirements Definition Document
- Review Program Flowchart
- Review System Conversion Plan
- Review System Conversion Checklist
- Review Data Conversion Plan
- Review Data Conversion Checklist
- Review Installation and Implementation Plan
- Review Installation and Implementation Test Checklist
- Review System Upgrade Checklist
- Update User Manual
- Update Desk Procedures
- Update Computer Operator Manual

- Update Standards and Guidelines Manual
- Update Disaster Recovery Plan
- Prepare Dataflow Diagrams
- Complete File Description Form

1.4.1.3 METHODS ANALYSTS

- Review System Conversion Plan
- Review Installation and Implementation Plan
- Update User Manual
- Update Desk Procedures
- Update Computer Operator Manual
- Refer to Statistical Quality-Control Graphs
- Refer to Statistical Quality-Control Checklist
- Update Standards and Guidelines Manual
- Update Disaster Recovery Plan

1.4.2 SUPERVISOR OF PROGRAMMING

- Prepares System Conversion Plan
- Reviews and approves Installation and Implementation Plan
- Reviews Programming Checklist
- Approves Software Version Form
- Reviews Patch Request Form
- Prepares Organization Charts

1.4.2.1 SYSTEMS PROGRAMMERS

- Review Record Layout Form
- Review File Description Form
- Review Structure Chart
- Review and update Nassi–Shneiderman Charts
- Review and revise Program Flowchart
- Review and revise System Flowchart
- Review and revise Detail Design Document
- Review System Conversion Plan
- Review Data-Flow Diagrams
- Refer to System Conversion Checklist

- Refer to Installation and Implementation Plan
- Refer to Installation and Implementation Package Form
- Refer to Installation and Implementation Test Checklist
- Prepare Programming Checklist
- Approve Software Version Form
- Complete Patch Request Form
- Review or revise Runbook Checklist
- Refer to User Manual

1.4.2.2 APPLICATION PROGRAMMERS

- Review Record Layout Form
- Review File Description Form
- Review Structure Chart
- Review and revise Nassi–Shneiderman Charts
- Review and revise Program Flowchart
- Review and revise System Flowchart
- Review Report Layout Form
- Review and revise Detail Design Document
- Review System Conversion Plan
- Refer to System Conversion Checklist
- Refer to Installation and Implementation Plan
- Refer to Installation and Implementation Package Form
- Refer to Installation and Implementation Test Checklist
- Review Data-Flow Diagrams
- Prepare Programming Checklist
- Approve Software Version Form
- Complete Patch Request Form
- Review or revise Runbook Checklist
- Refer to User Manual

1.5 MANAGER OF SUBCONTRACT SUPPORT

- Prepares Organization Charts
- Prepares and approves Request for Proposal Plan
- Reviews and approves Subcontractor Requirements List Form

1.6 PROJECT MANAGER

- References Feasibility Study Document
- References Cost–Benefit Analysis Document
- Prepares and approves Statement of Work
- Reviews Data Dictionary
- Reviews Data Model
- Reviews Structured English
- Reviews Data-Flow Diagrams
- Reviews and approves Requirements Definition Document
- Reviews and approves Alternatives Analysis Document
- Reviews and approves Functional Specifications Document
- Reviews Database Specifications Document
- Reviews Record Layouts Form
- Reviews File Description Form
- Reviews Structure Chart Checklist
- Reviews Nassi–Shneiderman Charts
- Reviews Program Flowchart
- Reviews Systems Flowchart
- Reviews Report Layout Form
- Reviews Database Design Flowcharts
- Reviews and approves Preliminary Design Document
- Reviews and approves Detail Design Document
- Reviews Decision Table
- Reviews Decision Tree
- Reviews and approves Test Plan
- Reviews and approves Test Report Form
- Reviews Hierarchy Input–Process–Output (HIPO) Documentation
- Reviews and approves Verification/Validation Plan
- Reviews Subsystem Test Report Form
- Reviews System Test Report Form
- Reviews and approves System Conversion Plan
- Reviews and approves Data Conversion Plan
- Reviews and approves Installation and Implementation Plan
- Reviews Installation and Implementation Package Form
- Reviews Data Center—Operations Plan
- Reviews Data Center—Operations Checklist
- Reviews User Manual

- Reviews Computer Operator Manual
- Reviews and approves Training Plan
- Reviews Instructor's Guide
- Reviews Student Handout
- Reviews and approves Training Schedule Form
- Reviews and approves Configuration Management Plan
- Reviews and approves Software Quality-Assurance Plan
- Prepares Project Plan
- Prepares and reviews Bar (Gantt) Chart
- Generates and reviews Activity Relationship Report Form
- Develops and reviews Network Diagrams
- Develops and reviews Work Breakdown Structure
- Generates and reviews Resource Histogram
- Prepares Organization Charts
- Completes and reviews Status Update Form
- Completes and reviews Resource Usage Report Form
- Generates and reviews Resource Usage Form
- Generates and reviews Project Schedule Report Form
- Prepares and reviews Monthly Status Report Form
- Generates and reviews Project Cost Report Form
- Generates and reviews "S" Cost Curve
- Prepares and reviews Directives Checklist
- Reviews and approves Request for Proposal Plan
- Reviews Subcontractor Requirements List Form

2.0 STEERING COMMITTEE

- Reviews Statement of Work
- Reviews Project Plan
- Reviews Monthly Status Report Form
- Reviews Feasibility Study Document

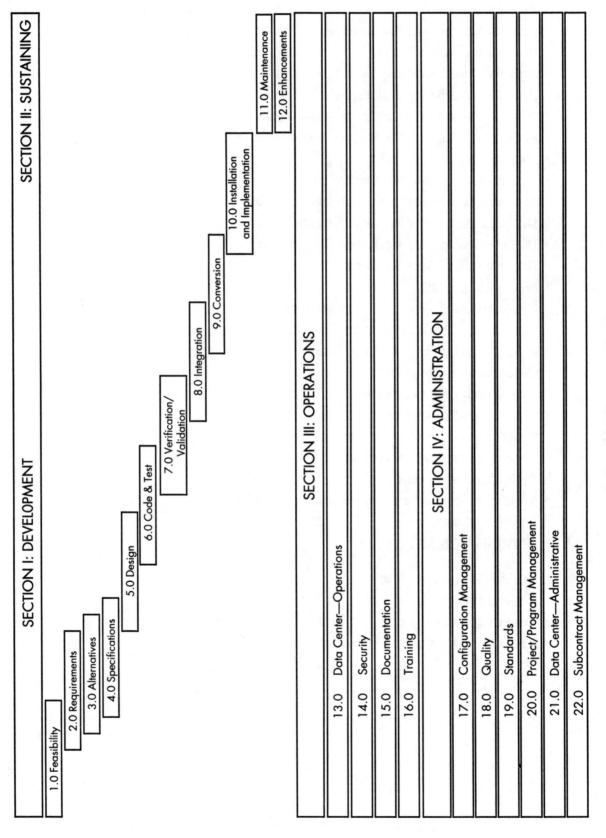

SECTION I: DEVELOPMENT

SECTION II: SUSTAINING

1.0 Feasibility

2.0 Requirements

3.0 Alternatives

4.0 Specifications

5.0 Design

6.0 Code & Test

7.0 Verification/Validation

8.0 Integration

9.0 Conversion

10.0 Installation and Implementation

11.0 Maintenance

12.0 Enhancements

SECTION III: OPERATIONS

13.0   Data Center—Operations

14.0   Security

15.0   Documentation

16.0   Training

SECTION IV: ADMINISTRATION

17.0   Configuration Management

18.0   Quality

19.0   Standards

20.0   Project/Program Management

21.0   Data Center—Administrative

22.0   Subcontract Management

SOFTWARE LIFE CYCLE CHART

SOFTWARE LIFE CYCLE CHART

1.0 FEASIBILITY

- Develop Feasibility Study Document
- Develop Statement of Work
- Complete Manual-Checkout Form

2.0 REQUIREMENTS

- Develop Data Dictionary
- Develop Structured English
- Develop Data-Flow Diagrams
- Develop Process Activation Table
- Develop Process Specification
- Complete Prototyping Checklist
- Develop Requirements Definition Document
- Complete Record Layout Form
- Complete File Description Form
- Complete Software Ergonomics Checklist
- Complete Report Layout Form
- Develop Decision Table
- Develop Decision Tree
- Develop Test Plan
- Develop Verification/Validation Plan
- Complete and update Manual-Checkout Form
- Develop Request for Proposal Plan
- Complete and update Subcontractor Requirements List Form
- Develop Data Models
- Complete Software Ergonomics Checklist
- Complete System Access Controls Checklist

3.0 ALTERNATIVES

- Develop Cost–Benefit Analysis Document
- Develop Data-Flow Diagrams
- Develop Process Specification

- Complete Prototyping Checklist
- Review Requirements Definition Document
- Develop and refer to Systems Flowchart
- Develop and refer to Decision Table
- Develop and refer to Decision Tree
- Develop Test Plan
- Review and update Verification/Validation Plan
- Complete and update Manual-Checkout Form
- Complete and update Request for Proposal Plan
- Complete and update Subcontractor Requirements List Form
- Prepare Alternatives Analysis Document

4.0 SPECIFICATIONS

- Develop Data-Flow Diagrams
- Develop Process Activation Table
- Develop Process Specification
- Complete Prototyping Checklist
- Review Requirements Definition Document
- Review Alternatives Analysis Document
- Develop and refer to File Description Form
- Develop and refer to Record Layout Form
- Complete System/Subsystem Specifications Checklist
- Develop Database Specifications Document
- Complete Software Ergonomics Checklist
- Develop Database Design Flowcharts
- Develop Test Plan
- Review and update Verification/Validation Plan
- Develop System Conversion Plan
- Complete System Conversion Checklist
- Develop Data Conversion Plan
- Complete Data Conversion Checklist
- Develop Data Center—Operations Plan
- Complete Data Center—Operations Checklist
- Develop Configuration Management Plan
- Complete and update File Archive Form
- Complete and update File Request Form
- Develop Software Quality-Assurance Plan

- Complete and update Maintenance Control Report
- Complete and update Manual-Checkout Form
- Complete Runbook Checklist
- Complete Software Ergonomics Checklist

5.0 DESIGN

- Review and update Data Dictionary
- Review Data Models
- Develop and review Structured English
- Refer to Data-Flow Diagrams
- Refer to Process Activation Table
- Refer to Process Specification
- Complete Prototyping Checklist
- Refer to Requirements Definition Document
- Refer to Functional Specifications Document
- Develop and refer to Database Specifications Document
- Refer to Record Layout Form
- Refer to File Description Form
- Develop Structure Chart
- Develop and refer to System Flowchart
- Develop Database Design Flowcharts
- Develop Preliminary Design Document
- Develop Decision Table
- Develop Decision Tree
- Develop and refer to Test Plan
- Review and update Verification/Validation Plan
- Review and update System Conversion Plan
- Refer to and update System Conversion Checklist
- Review and update Data Conversion Plan
- Refer to and update Data Conversion Checklist
- Develop Installation and Implementation Plan
- Complete Installation and Implementation Test Checklist
- Review and update Data Center—Operations Plan
- Complete and update Data Center—Operations Checklist
- Review and update Configuration Management Plan
- Complete Problem Report Form and Flowchart
- Complete and update File Archive Form

- Complete and update File Request Form
- Complete and update Software Quality-Assurance Plan
- Complete and update Maintenance Control Report
- Complete and update Manual-Checkout Form
- Complete Runbook Checklist

6.0 CODE AND TEST

- Refer to and update Data Dictionary
- Develop and refer to Structured English
- Refer to Data-Flow Diagrams
- Refer to Process Activation Table
- Refer to Process Specification
- Complete Prototyping Checklist
- Refer to Requirements Definition Document
- Refer to Functional Specifications Document
- Complete and update Database Specifications Document
- Develop Record Layout Form
- Complete File Description Form
- Refer to Structure Chart
- Develop Nassi–Shneiderman Charts
- Develop Program Flowchart
- Refer to Systems Flowchart
- Refer to Preliminary Design Document
- Develop Detail Design Document
- Develop and refer to Decision Table
- Develop and refer to Decision Tree
- Develop Test Plan
- Develop Test Report Form
- Develop Hierarchy Input–Process–Output (HIPO) Documentation
- Review and update Verification/Validation Plan
- Review and update System Conversion Plan
- Refer to and update System Conversion Checklist
- Review and update Data Conversion Plan
- Refer to and update Data Conversion Checklist
- Review and update Installation and Implementation Plan
- Refer to and update Installation and Implementation Test Checklist
- Review and update Data Center—Operations Plan

- Complete and update System Utilization Log Form
- Complete and update Machine-Run Log Form
- Complete and update System Incidence Log Form
- Complete and update Software Program Requirement Log Form
- Complete and update Software Program Distribution Form
- Complete and update Data Center—Operations Checklist
- Review and update Configuration Management Plan
- Complete and update Problem Report Form and Flowchart
- Complete and update File Archive Form
- Complete and update File Request Form
- Complete and update Patch Request Form
- Complete and update Maintenance Control Report Form
- Complete and update Manual-Checkout Form
- Complete and update Runbook Checklist
- Complete and update Tape-Reel Archive Form
- Complete and update Scratch-Tape Reuse Form
- Complete and update Performance Validation Checklist
- Refer to Data Models

7.0 VERIFICATION/VALIDATION

- Refer to Decision Table
- Refer to Decision Tree
- Refer to Test Plan
- Complete and update Test Report Form
- Complete Verification/Validation Plan
- Develop Verification/Validation Test Completion Report Form
- Complete Verification/Validation Test Checklist
- Review and update System Conversion Plan
- Refer to and update System Conversion Checklist
- Review and update Data Conversion Plan
- Refer to and update Data Conversion Checklist
- Review and update Installation and Implementation Plan
- Refer to and update Installation and Implementation Test Checklist
- Review and update Data Center—Operations Plan
- Complete and update System Utilization Log Form
- Complete and update Machine-Run Log Form
- Complete and update System Incidence Log Form

- Complete and update Software Program Requirement Log Form
- Complete and update Software Program Distribution Form
- Complete and update Data Center—Operations Checklist
- Review and update Configuration Management Plan
- Complete and update Software Version Form
- Complete and update Problem Report Form and Flowchart
- Complete Configuration Audit Checklist
- Complete and update File Archive Form
- Complete and update File Request Form
- Complete and update Patch Request Form
- Complete and update Maintenance Control Report Form
- Complete and update Manual-Checkout Form
- Complete and update Runbook Checklist
- Complete and update Tape-Reel Archive Form
- Complete and update Scratch-Tape Reuse Form
- Complete and update Performance Validation Checklist
- Refer to Structured English
- Refer to Dataflow Diagrams
- Refer to Requirements Definition Document
- Refer to Software Ergonomics Checklist
- Refer to System Access Controls Checklist

8.0 INTEGRATION

- Refer to Requirements Definition Document
- Complete and update Test Report Form
- Complete and update Verification/Validation Test Completion Report Form
- Complete and update Subsystem Test Report Form
- Complete and update System Test Report Form
- Review and update System Conversion Plan
- Refer to and update System Conversion Checklist
- Review and update Data Conversion Plan
- Refer to and update Data Conversion Checklist
- Review and update Installation and Implementation Plan
- Refer to and update Installation and Implementation Test Checklist
- Review and update Data Center—Operations Plan
- Complete and update System Utilization Log Form
- Complete and update Machine-Run Log Form

- Complete and update System Incidence Log Form
- Complete and update Software Program Requirement Log Form
- Complete and update Software Program Distribution Form
- Complete and update Data Center—Operations Checklist
- Review and update Configuration Management Plan
- Complete and update Software Version Form
- Complete and update Problem Report Form and Flowchart
- Refer to and update Configuration Audit Checklist
- Complete and update File Archive Form
- Complete and update File Request Form
- Complete and update Patch Request Form
- Complete and update Maintenance Control Report Form
- Complete and update Manual-Checkout Form
- Complete and update Runbook Checklist
- Complete and update Tape-Reel Archive Form
- Complete and update Scratch-Tape Reuse Form
- Complete and update Performance Validation Checklist

9.0 CONVERSION

- Complete and update Test Report Form
- Complete and update Verification/Validation Test Completion Report Form
- Complete and update Subsystem Test Report Form
- Complete and update System Test Report Form
- Complete and update System Conversion Plan
- Refer to and update System Conversion Checklist
- Complete and update Data Conversion Plan
- Refer to and update Data Conversion Checklist
- Review and update Installation and Implementation Plan
- Refer to and update Installation and Implementation Test Checklist
- Review and update Data Center—Operations Plan
- Complete and update System Utilization Log Form
- Complete and update Machine-Run Log Form
- Complete and update System Incidence Log Form
- Complete and update Software Program Requirement Log Form
- Complete and update Software Program Distribution Form
- Complete and update Data Center—Operations Checklist
- Complete and update Configuration Management Plan

- Complete and update Software Version Form
- Complete and update Problem Report Form and Flowchart
- Refer to and update Configuration Audit Checklist
- Complete and update File Archive Form
- Complete and update File Request Form
- Complete and update Patch Request Form
- Complete and update Maintenance Control Report Form
- Complete and update Manual-Checkout Form
- Complete and update Runbook Checklist
- Complete and update Tape-Reel Archive Form
- Complete and update Scratch-Tape Reuse Form
- Complete and update Performance Validation Checklist

10.0 INSTALLATION AND IMPLEMENTATION

- Complete and update Test Report Form
- Complete and update Verification/Validation Test Completion Report Form
- Complete and update Subsystem Test Report Form
- Complete and update System Test Report Form
- Complete and update Installation and Implementation Plan
- Complete and update Installation and Implementation Package Form
- Refer to and update Installation and Implementation Test Checklist
- Complete Programming Checklist
- Complete Facility Usage Checklist
- Complete System Performance Graphs
- Complete System Productivity Graphs
- Complete and update Data Center—Operations Plan
- Complete and update System Utilization Log Form
- Complete and update Machine-Run Log Form
- Complete and update System Incidence Log Form
- Complete and update Software Program Requirement Log Form
- Complete and update Software Program Distribution Form
- Complete and update Data Center—Operations Checklist
- Complete and update Software Version Form
- Complete and update Problem Report Form and Flowchart
- Refer to and update Configuration Audit Checklist
- Complete and update File Archive Form
- Complete and update File Request Form

- Complete and update Patch Request Form
- Complete and update Maintenance Control Report
- Complete and update Manual-Checkout Form
- Complete and update Runbook Checklist
- Complete and update Tape-Reel Archive Form
- Complete and update Scratch-Tape Reuse Form
- Complete and update Performance Validation Checklist

11.0 MAINTENANCE

- Refer to and update Data-Flow Diagrams
- Refer to and update Process Activation Table
- Refer to and update Process Specification
- Refer to and update Requirements Definition Document
- Complete and update Record Layout Form
- Complete and update File Description Form
- Refer to and update Structure Chart
- Refer to and update Nassi–Shneiderman Charts
- Refer to and update Program Flowchart
- Refer to and update Systems Flowchart
- Refer to and update Report Layout Form
- Refer to and update Preliminary Design Document
- Refer to and update Detail Design Document
- Refer to and update Decision Table
- Refer to and update Decision Tree
- Refer to and update Hierarchy–Input–Process–Output (HIPO) Documentation
- Complete and update Installation and Implementation Package Form
- Refer to and update Programming Checklist
- Refer to and update Facility Usage Checklist
- Complete and update Equipment Maintenance Report Form
- Complete System Upgrade Checklist
- Refer to and update System Performance Graphs
- Refer to and update System Productivity Graphs
- Complete and update System Utilization Log Form
- Complete and update Machine-Run Log Form
- Complete and update System Incidence Log Form
- Complete and update Software Program Requirement Log Form

- Complete and update Software Program Distribution Form
- Complete and update Software Version Form
- Complete and update Problem Report Form and Flowchart
- Complete and update File Archive Form
- Complete and update File Request Form
- Complete and update Patch Request Form
- Complete and update Maintenance Control Report Form
- Complete Quality-Circles Plan
- Complete Quality-Circles Checklist
- Complete and update Statistical Quality-Control Graphs
- Complete Statistical Quality-Control Checklist
- Complete and update Manual-Checkout Form
- Complete and update Runbook Checklist
- Complete and update Tape-Reel Archive Form
- Complete and update Scratch-Tape Reuse Form
- Complete and update Performance Validation Checklist
- Complete and update System Access Controls Checklist

12.0 ENHANCEMENTS

- Refer to and update Data-Flow Diagrams
- Refer to and update Process Activation Table
- Refer to and update Process Specification
- Refer to and update Requirements Definition Document
- Refer to and update Record Layout Form
- Refer to and update File Description Form
- Refer to and update Structure Chart Checklist
- Refer to and update Nassi–Shneiderman Charts
- Refer to and update Program Flowchart
- Refer to and update Systems Flowchart
- Refer to and update Report Layout Form
- Refer to and update Preliminary Design Document
- Refer to and update Detail Design Document
- Refer to and update Decision Table
- Refer to and update Decision Tree
- Refer to and update Hierarchy–Input–Process–Output (HIPO) Documentation
- Complete and update Installation and Implementation Package Form

- Refer to and update Equipment Maintenance Report Form
- Refer to and update System Upgrade Checklist
- Refer to and update System Performance Graphs
- Refer to and update System Productivity Graphs
- Complete and update System Utilization Log Form
- Complete and update Machine-Run Log Form
- Complete and update System Incidence Log Form
- Complete and update Software Program Requirement Log Form
- Complete and update Software Program Distribution Form
- Complete and update Software Version Form
- Complete and update Problem Report Form and Flowchart
- Complete and update File Archive Form
- Complete and update File Request Form
- Complete and update Patch Request Form
- Complete and update Maintenance Control Report Form
- Complete and update Quality-Circles Plan
- Refer to and update Quality-Circles Checklist
- Complete and update Statistical Quality-Control Graphs
- Refer to and update Statistical Quality-Control Checklist
- Complete and update Manual-Checkout Form
- Complete and update Runbook Checklist
- Complete and update Tape-Reel Archive Form
- Complete and update Scratch-Tape Reuse Form
- Complete and update Performance Validation Checklist
- Refer to and update System Access Controls Checklist

13.0   DATA CENTER—OPERATIONS

- Develop Data Center—Operations Plan
- Complete System Utilization Log Form
- Complete Machine-Run Log Form
- Complete System Incidence Log Form
- Complete Software Program Requirement Log Form
- Complete Software Program Distribution Form
- Complete Data Center—Operations Checklist

14.0 SECURITY

- Develop Audit Plan
- Complete Computing Facility Controls Checklist
- Complete Systems Access Controls Checklist

15.0 DOCUMENTATION

- Develop, refer to, and update User Manual
- Develop, refer to, and update Desk Procedures
- Develop, refer to, and update Computer Operator Manual

16.0 TRAINING

- Develop, refer to, and update Training Plan
- Develop, refer to, and update Instructor's Guide
- Develop, refer to, and update Student Handout
- Develop, refer to, and update Training Schedule Form

17.0 CONFIGURATION MANAGEMENT

- Develop, refer to, and update Configuration Management Plan
- Develop, refer to, and update Software Version Form
- Refer to and update Problem Report Form
- Complete Configuration Audit Checklist
- Develop, refer to, and update File Archive Form
- Refer to File Request Form
- Refer to and update Patch Request Form

18.0 QUALITY

- Develop, refer to, and update Software Quality-Assurance Plan
- Complete Maintenance Control Report Form
- Develop, refer to, and update Quality-Circles Plan
- Complete Quality-Circles Checklist
- Refer to and update Statistical Quality Control Graphs
- Complete Statistical Quality-Control Checklist

19.0 STANDARDS

- Develop, refer to, and update Standards and Guidelines Manual
- Develop, refer to, and update Disaster Recovery Plan
- Complete Risk Assessment Checklist
- Complete Software Documentation Checklist

20.0 PROJECT/PROGRAM MANAGEMENT

- Develop, refer to, and update Project Plan
- Develop, refer to, and update Bar (Gantt) Chart
- Develop, refer to, and update Activity Relationship Report Form
- Develop, refer to, and update Network Diagram
- Develop, refer to, and update Work Breakdown Structure
- Develop, refer to, and update Resource Histogram
- Develop, refer to, and update Organization Charts
- Complete Status Update Form
- Develop, refer to, and update Resource Usage Report Form
- Develop, refer to, and update Project Schedule Report Form
- Develop, refer to, and update Monthly Status Report Form
- Develop, refer to, and update Project Cost Report Form
- Develop, refer to, and update "S" Cost Curve
- Complete Directives Checklist

21.0 DATA CENTER—ADMINISTRATIVE

- Develop, refer to, and update Manual-Checkout Form
- Complete Runbook Checklist
- Develop, refer to, and update Tape-Reel Archive Form
- Develop, refer to, and update Scratch-Tape Reuse Form

22.0 SUBCONTRACT MANAGEMENT

- Develop, refer to, and update Request for Proposal Plan
- Complete Subcontractor Requirements List Form
- Develop, refer to, and update Performance Validation Checklist

SECTION I
DEVELOPMENT

Chapter 1

Feasibility

FEASIBILITY STUDY DOCUMENT OVERVIEW

I. DESCRIPTION

- Records the analysis conducted to determine whether a computer solution to a problem or circumstance is practical

II. OBJECTIVES

- Reduce money wasted on needless or impractical projects
- Reduce the risk incurred in attempting a project
- Define the goals and objectives of a future project

III. ORGANIZATION

- Refer to Manager of Development (1.1), Project Manager (1.6), and Steering Committee (2.0) in the Organization and Responsibilities Chart

IV. SCHEDULE

- Refer to the Feasibility phase (1.0) of the Software Life Cycle Chart

FEASIBILITY STUDY DOCUMENT

   I. Present title page, which includes:
- A. Document title
- B. Document number
- C. Original release date
- D. Current release date
- E. Current revision number
- F. Appropriate signatures and date

  II. Present modifications sheet, which includes:
- A. Sequentially numbered list of changes
- B. Explanation of changes
- C. Page numbers of changes
- D. Appropriate signatures and date

 III. Present table of contents, which includes:
- A. Section headings
- B. Chapter titles
- C. Chapter subtitles
- D. Relevant page numbers

 IV. Present executive summary, which includes:
- A. Overview
- B. Principal points

  V. Present introduction, which includes:
- A. Goals
- B. Scope
- C. Objectives, like:
  - Technical
  - Business
- D. Background information

 VI. State the problem, which includes:
- A. Description
- B. History of dysfunctional behavior

VII. Describe the current environment, which includes:
  A. Organization
  B. Equipment
  C. Hardware
  D. Statistics
  E. Functions
  F. Constraints, limitations, and special considerations
    • Throughput
    • Volume
  G. Assumptions
  H. Data structure and flow
  I. Software
  J. Workload

VIII. For each possible solution, provide:
  A. Technical description, which includes:
    • Hardware
    • Software
  B. Operational description, which includes:
    • Resources
    • Procedures
    • Schedule
  C. Financial description, which includes:
    • Direct versus indirect costs
    • Fixed versus variable costs
    • Recurring versus nonrecurring costs
    • Break-even point
  D. Advantages, which include:
    • Monetary
    • Value-added
  E. Disadvantages, which include:
    • Monetary
    • Nonmonetary
  F. Assumptions
  G. Constraints, limitations, and special considerations

IX. Make recommendations

X. Prepare glossary

XI. Attach appendixes

COST–BENEFIT ANALYSIS DOCUMENT OVERVIEW

I. DESCRIPTION

- Provides an objective cost appraisal of each alternative in the Alternatives Analysis Document

II. OBJECTIVES

- Record for future reference the financial impact of each alternative
- Provide useful information to include in the Alternatives Analysis Document (often appended to that document)

III. ORGANIZATION

- Refer to Systems Analysts (1.1.1.2), Methods Analysts (1.1.1.3), and Project Manager (1.6) in the Organization and Responsibilities Chart

IV. SCHEDULE

- Refer to the Alternatives Analysis phase (3.0) of the Software Life Cycle Chart

COST–BENEFIT ANALYSIS DOCUMENT

I. Present title page, which includes:
    A. Document title
    B. Document number
    C. Original release date
    D. Current release date
    E. Current revision number
    F. Appropriate signatures and date

II. Present modifications sheet, which includes:
    A. Sequentially numbered list of changes
    B. Explanation of changes
    C. Page numbers of changes
    D. Appropriate signatures and date

III. Present table of contents, which includes:
    A. Section headings
    B. Chapter titles
    C. Chapter subtitles
    D. Relevant page numbers

IV. Present executive summary, which includes:
    A. Overview
    B. Principal points

V. Present introduction, which includes:
    A. Goals
    B. Scope
    C. Objectives, like:
        • Technical
        • Business
    D. Background information

VI. Provide Feasibility Study Document or Alternatives Analysis Document overview, which includes:
    A. Background information

B. Status
C. Cost
D. Schedule
E. Current environment
F. Alternatives

VII. Present evaluation criteria, which include:
    A. Assumptions
    B. Constraints and limitations
    C. Special considerations
    D. Criteria, which include:
       • Development
       • Implementation
       • Operating
    E. Costs, which include:
       • Development
       • Implementation
       • Operating

VIII. Present cost-calculation methods, which include:
    A. System life cycle costs
    B. Present value cost
    C. Residual value estimates
    D. Net present value
    E. Benefit/cost ratio
    F. Payback period

IX. Provide cost–benefit comparison among alternatives

X. Make recommendations

XI. Attach appendixes

STATEMENT OF WORK OVERVIEW

I. DESCRIPTION

- An agreement between the project manager and the user that defines the terms and conditions for conducting and completing a project

II. OBJECTIVES

- Facilitate more reliable planning
- Define major responsibilities
- Identify major resource requirements
- Specify significant tasks and deliverables
- Reduce the chance for miscommunication

III. ORGANIZATION

- Refer to Manager of Development (1.1), Supervisor of Analysis (1.1.1), Supervisor of Design (1.1.2), Supervisor of Programming (1.1.3), Project Manager (1.6), and Steering Committee (2.0) in the Organization and Responsibilities Chart

IV. SCHEDULE

- Refer to the Feasibility phase (1.0) of the Software Life Cycle Chart

STATEMENT OF WORK

I. Prepare introduction, which includes:
   A. Background information
   B. Goals and objectives
   C. Special requirements, constraints and limitations, related to:
      • Technical
      • Operational
      • Economic
   D. References, which include:
      • Laws
      • Regulations
      • Policies
      • Procedures

II. Describe product, which includes:
   A. Overall description
   B. Component listing and accompanying descriptions

III. Describe deliverables, which include:
   A. Listings, like:
      • Hardware
      • Software
      • Documentation
      • Services
   B. Description of each

IV. Describe performance requirements, which include:
   A. Throughput
   B. Volume
   C. Response time

V. Describe responsibilities, which include:
   A. Technical responsibilities, like:
      • Analysis
      • Design

- Construction
- Implementation

B. Administrative responsibilities, like:
- Scheduling
- Statusing
- Reporting
- Change control
- Budgeting
- Resource allocation
- Reviews

VI. Describe acceptance criteria, which include:
   A. Technical
   B. Operational
   C. Economic

VII. List approvals

VIII. Attach appendixes

Chapter 2

Requirements

DATA DICTIONARY OVERVIEW

I. DESCRIPTION

- Defines data in terms of meaning, format, and usage

II. OBJECTIVES

- Improve communication
- Provide consistency in the usage of data
- Enable a better understanding of a system (whether manual, automated, or both)
- Serve as a resource for subsequent development phases, including Design, and Code and Test

III. ORGANIZATION

- Refer to Database Analysts (1.1.1.1), Systems Analysts (1.1.1.2), Systems Designers (1.1.2.1), Systems Programmers (1.1.3.1), Application Programmers (1.1.3.2), Database Administrators (1.2.3), and Project Manager (1.6) in the Organization and Responsibilities Chart

IV. SCHEDULE

- Refer to the Requirements (2.0), Design (5.0), Code and Test (6.0), and Verification/Validation (7.0) phases of the Software Life Cycle Chart

DATA DICTIONARY

ACCUMULATED TIME CARD STATISTICS =

(TOTAL REGULAR HOURS + REGULAR HOURLY RATE + TOTAL OVERTIME HOURS + OVERTIME HOURLY RATES + TOTAL LEAVE WITH PAY HOURS PAID + TOTAL HOLIDAY HOURS PAID + TOTAL VACATION HOURS + PRETAX INVESTMENT PORTFOLIO AMOUNT)

TOTAL REGULAR HOURS WORKED = * THE CUMULATIVE HOURS WORKED FOR THE CURRENT PAY PERIOD.*

1(DIGIT)6   WITH THE DECIMAL POINT ONE POSITION TO THE RIGHT

REGULAR HOURLY RATE = * THE AMOUNT THAT THE EMPLOYEE RECEIVES FOR AN HOUR OF WORK.*

1(DIGIT)6   WITH THE DECIMAL POINT TWO POSITIONS FROM THE RIGHT

TOTAL OVERTIME HOURS = * THE CUMULATIVE HOURS WORKED ABOVE EIGHT HOURS PER DAY AT TIME AND A HALF AND DOUBLE TIME.*

1(DIGIT)6 WITH THE DECIMAL POINT ONE POSITION TO THE RIGHT

OVERTIME HOURLY RATE = * THE AMOUNT THAT AN EMPLOYEE RECEIVES FOR AN HOUR OF WORK OVER EIGHT HOURS PER DAY OR ON SELECTED HOLIDAYS AND WEEKENDS.*

1(DIGIT)6   WITH DECIMAL POINT TWO POSITIONS FROM THE RIGHT

TOTAL LEAVE WITH PAY = * THE AMOUNT OF MONEY THE EMPLOYEE RECEIVES EVEN THOUGH EMPLOYEE DID NOT WORK.*

1(DIGIT)6   WITH THE DECIMAL POINT TWO POSITIONS FROM THE RIGHT

TOTAL HOLIDAY HOURS PAID = * THE CUMULATIVE MONIES THAT THE EMPLOYEE IS ENTITLED TO DUE TO LEGAL HOLIDAYS.*

1(DIGIT)2   NO DECIMAL

TOTAL VACATION HOURS PAID = * THE CUMULATIVE MONIES THAT THE EMPLOYEE IS ENTITLED TO FOR VACATIONS.*

1(DIGIT)6   WITH THE DECIMAL POINT TWO POSITIONS FROM THE RIGHT

PRE-TAX INVESTMENT PORTFOLIO AMOUNT = * THE AMOUNT TO BE DEDUCTED FROM THE TOTAL PAY AND THAT IS NOT TO BE TAXED UNTIL WITHDRAWN AT A LATER DATE.*

1(DIGIT)6   WITH THE DECIMAL POINT TWO POSITIONS FROM THE RIGHT

DATA MODELS OVERVIEW

I. DESCRIPTION

- Shows the relationships among data in a system and their attributes

II. OBJECTIVES

- Stress the conceptual aspects of a database rather than its physical implementation
- Improve communication among users, analysts, and programmers
- Document the user's view of data for future reference

III. ORGANIZATION

- Refer to Database Analysts (1.1.1.1), Systems Analysts (1.1.1.2), Systems Librarians (1.2.1), Configuration Management Specialists (1.2.4), and Project Managers (1.6) in the Organization and Responsibilities Chart

IV. SCHEDULE

- Refer to the Requirements (2.0), Design (5.0), and Code and Test (6.0) phases of the Software Life Cycle Chart

DATA MODELS CHECKLIST

I. Identify the contents of each data model, including:
- ☐ Objects
- ☐ Relationships among objects

II. Identify the following for each object:
- ☐ Data characteristics
- ☐ Descriptor

WARNIER-ORR (DATA) DIAGRAM

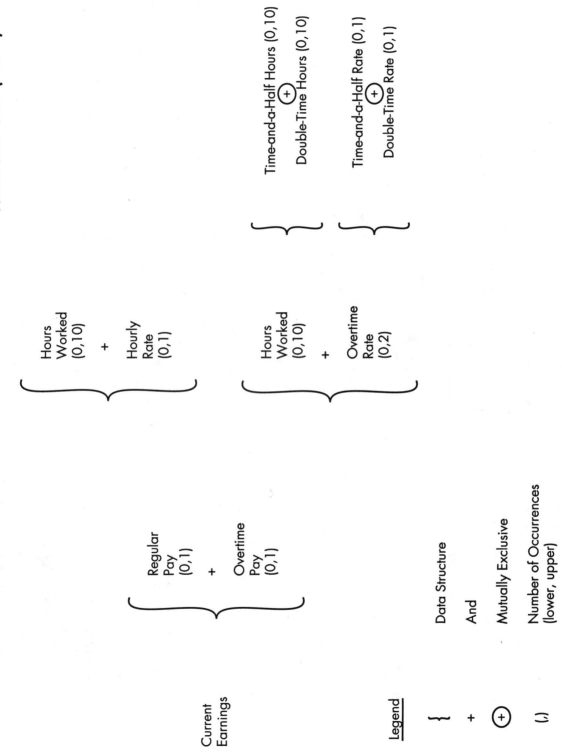

Current
Earnings
$\left\{ \begin{array}{l} \text{Regular} \\ \text{Pay} \\ (0,1) \\ + \\ \text{Overtime} \\ \text{Pay} \\ (0,1) \end{array} \right.$

$\left\{ \begin{array}{l} \text{Hours} \\ \text{Worked} \\ (0,10) \\ + \\ \text{Hourly} \\ \text{Rate} \\ (0,1) \end{array} \right.$

$\left\{ \begin{array}{l} \text{Hours} \\ \text{Worked} \\ (0,10) \\ + \\ \text{Overtime} \\ \text{Rate} \\ (0,2) \end{array} \right.$

$\left\{ \begin{array}{l} \text{Time-and-a-Half Hours } (0,10) \\ \oplus \\ \text{Double-Time Hours } (0,10) \end{array} \right.$

$\left\{ \begin{array}{l} \text{Time-and-a-Half Rate } (0,1) \\ \oplus \\ \text{Double-Time Rate } (0,1) \end{array} \right.$

Legend

{	Data Structure
+	And
⊕	Mutually Exclusive
(,)	Number of Occurrences (lower, upper)

ENTITY RELATIONSHIP DIAGRAM

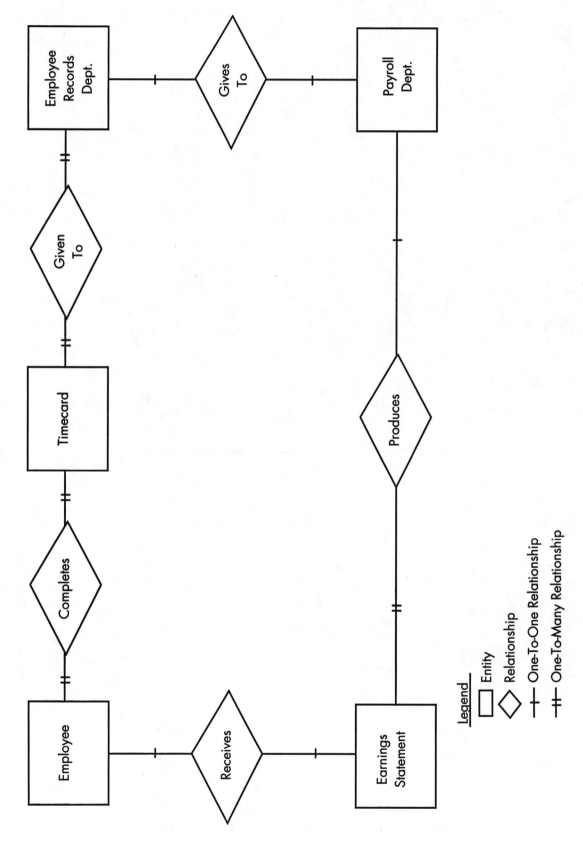

Legend

☐ Entity

◇ Relationship

┼ One-To-One Relationship

┼┼ One-To-Many Relationship

STRUCTURED ENGLISH OVERVIEW

I. DESCRIPTION

- Describes, using a natural language method, what occurs in a system; for example, what occurs in a functional primitive bubble in a Data-Flow Diagram, or the relationship between modules in a Structure Chart

II. OBJECTIVES

- Improve communication among project participants, such as among systems analysts, users, and programmers

III. ORGANIZATION

- Refer to Systems Analysts (1.1.1.2), Systems Designers (1.1.2.1), and Project Manager (1.6) in the Organization and Responsibilities Chart

IV. SCHEDULE

- Refer to the Requirements (2.0), Design (5.0), Code and Test (6.0), and Verification/Validation (7.0) phases of the Software Life Cycle Chart

PROCESS SPECIFICATION

2.7 COMPILE CURRENT EARNINGS FOR PAY PERIOD

For each employee sum:
- Regular hours pay amount

- Overtime pay amount

- Leave with pay amount

- Holiday pay amount

- Paid-vacation amount

Subtract pretax investment amount from sum to obtain current earnings

DATA-FLOW DIAGRAMS OVERVIEW

I. DESCRIPTION

- Displays the functions and data required for a system to operate

II. OBJECTIVES

- Illustrate the functions and subfunctions and required data using symbols rather than text, thereby facilitating comprehension
- Provide reference material for future development and sustaining activities
- Document requirements

III. ORGANIZATION

- Refer to Systems Analysts (1.1.1.2, 1.4.1.2), Systems Designers (1.1.2.1), Systems Programmers (1.1.3.1, 1.4.2.1), Application Programmers (1.1.3.2, 1.4.2.2), Configuration Management Specialists (1.2.4), and Project Manager (1.6) in the Organization and Responsibilities Chart

IV. SCHEDULE

- Refer to the Requirement (2.0), Alternatives (3.0), Specifications (4.0), Design (5.0), Code and Test (6.0), Verification/Validation (7.0), Maintenance (11.0), and Enhancements (12.0) phases of the Software Life Cycle Chart

PROCESS MODELING CHECKLIST

I. Determine technique to use, such as:
- ☐ Ward–Mellor
- ☐ Hatley–Pirbhai
- ☐ De Marco
- ☐ Gane and Sarson

II. For each process model in technique, determine:
- ☐ Functions
- ☐ Data repositories
- ☐ Flows of data
- ☐ Levels of decomposition

III. For each process in diagram, determine:
- ☐ Descriptor
- ☐ Numeric designator
- ☐ Input data
- ☐ Output data

WARD–MELLOR METHOD

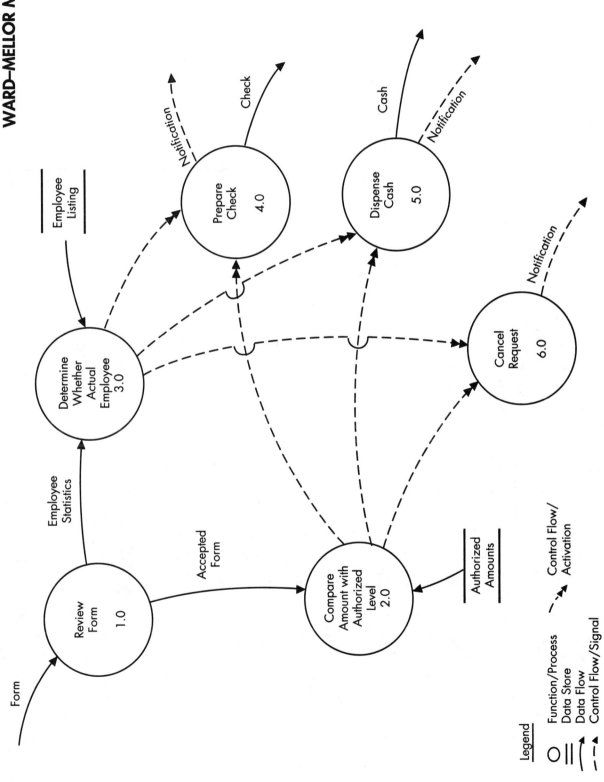

HATLEY—PIRBHAI METHOD

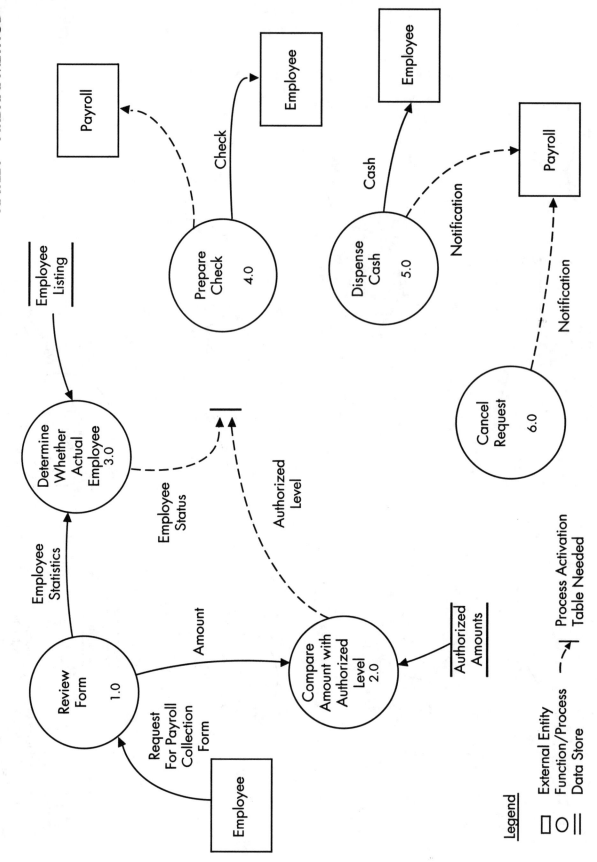

Legend

☐ External Entity
◯ Function/Process
▯ Data Store

⊣ Process Activation Table Needed

PROCESS ACTIVATION TABLE

Employee Status	Authorized Level	Process 4.0	Process 5.0	Process 6.0
True	True	1	0	0
	False	0	1	0
False	True	0	0	1
	False	0	0	1

Legend
0   Off
1   On

DE MARCO TECHNIQUE (CONTEXT LEVEL)

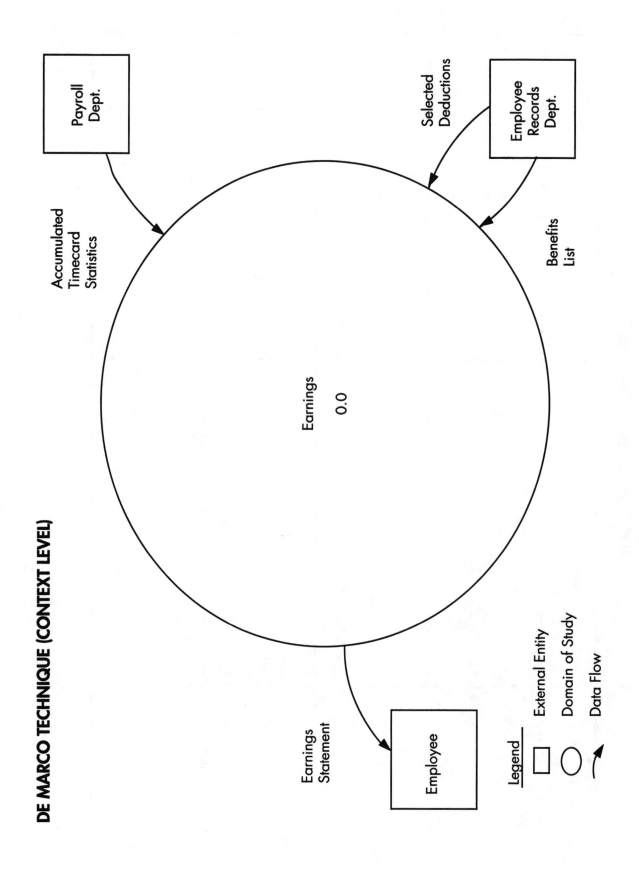

Payroll Dept.

Accumulated Timecard Statistics

Selected Deductions

Employee Records Dept.

Benefits List

Earnings
0.0

Earnings Statement

Employee

Legend

External Entity

Domain of Study

Data Flow

DE MARCO TECHNIQUE (MIDDLE LEVEL)

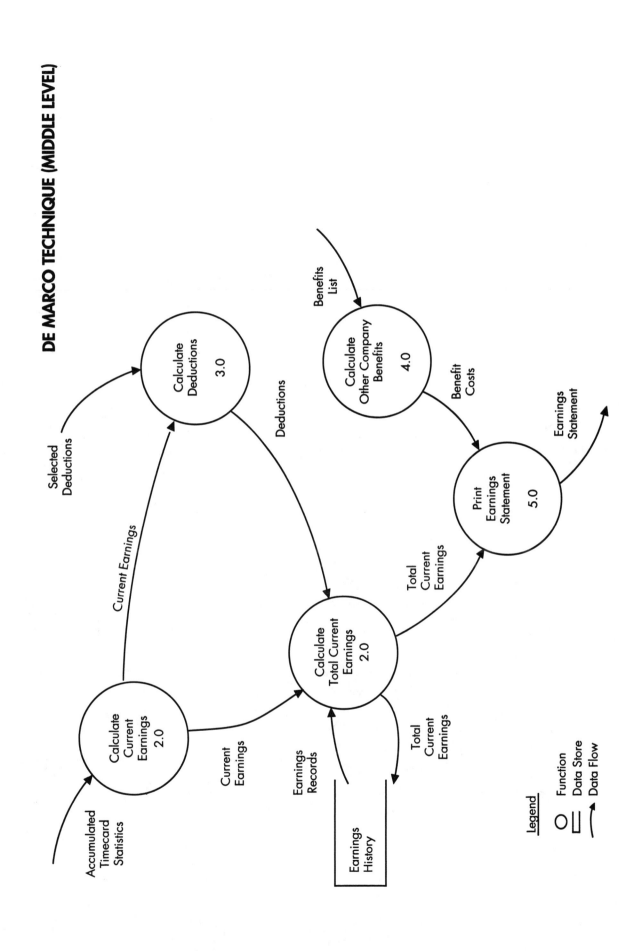

Legend

○ Function
⊏ Data Store
↱ Data Flow

DE MARCO TECHNIQUE (FUNCTIONAL PRIMITIVE LEVEL)

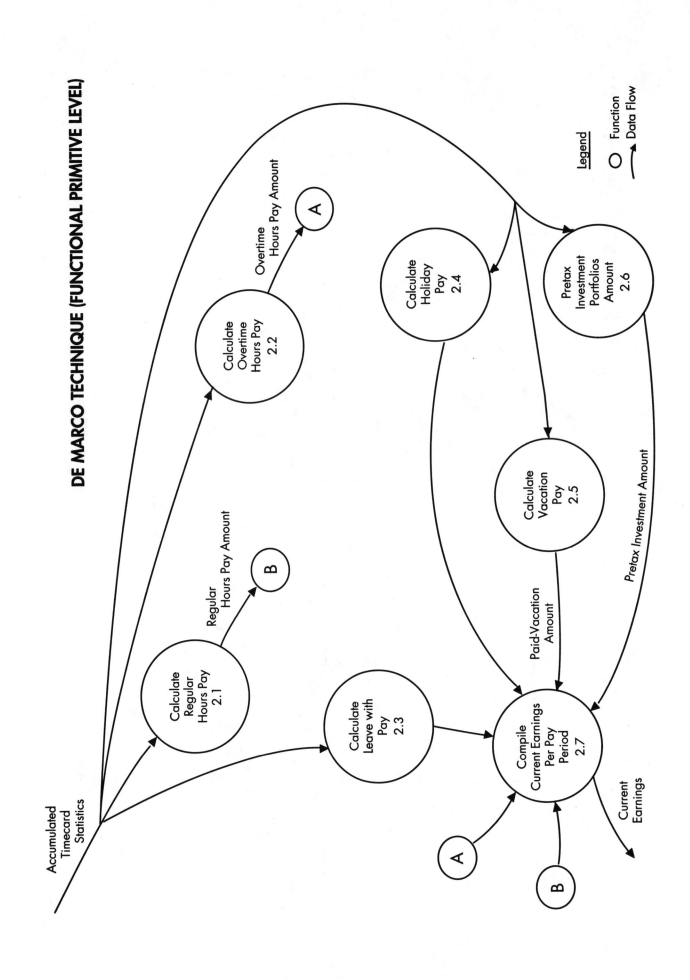

Accumulated Timecard Statistics

Calculate Regular Hours Pay 2.1

Regular Hours Pay Amount

B

Calculate Overtime Hours Pay 2.2

Overtime Hours Pay Amount

A

Calculate Leave with Pay 2.3

Calculate Holiday Pay 2.4

Calculate Vacation Pay 2.5

Pretax Investment Portfolios Amount 2.6

Paid-Vacation Amount

Pretax Investment Amount

Compile Current Earnings Per Pay Period 2.7

A

B

Current Earnings

Legend

○ Function

Data Flow

GANE AND SARSON TECHNIQUE
(MIDDLE LEVEL)

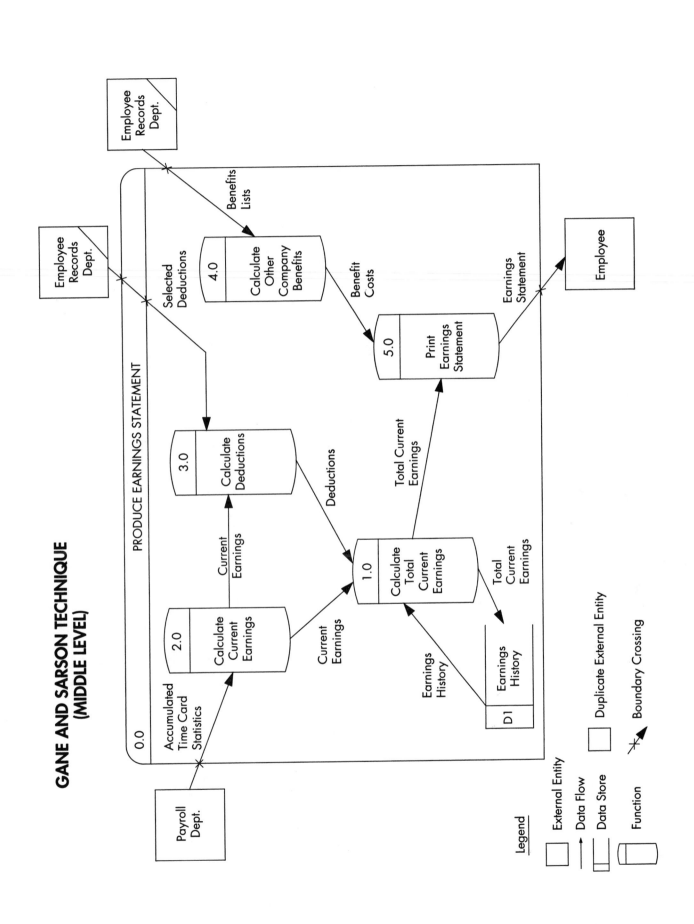

GANE AND SARSON TECHNIQUE
(EXPLODED)

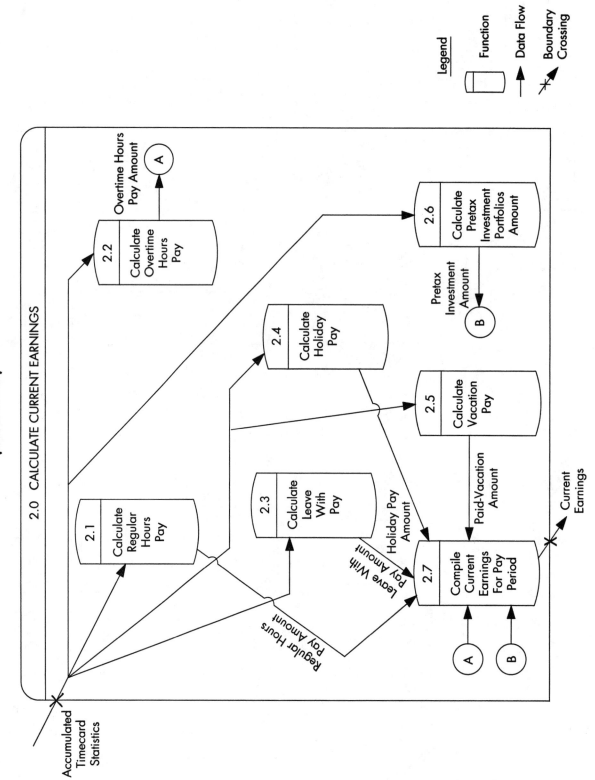

2.0   CALCULATE CURRENT EARNINGS

Accumulated Timecard Statistics

2.1 Calculate Regular Hours Pay

2.2 Calculate Overtime Hours Pay

Overtime Hours Pay Amount

A

2.3 Calculate Leave With Pay

2.4 Calculate Holiday Pay

2.5 Calculate Vacation Pay

2.6 Calculate Pretax Investment Portfolios Amount

Pretax Investment Amount

B

2.7 Compile Current Earnings For Pay Period

Regular Hours Pay Amount

Leave With Pay Amount

Holiday Pay Amount

Paid-Vacation Amount

Current Earnings

A

B

Legend

Function

Data Flow

Boundary Crossing

WARNIER–ORR TECHNIQUE (PROCESS)

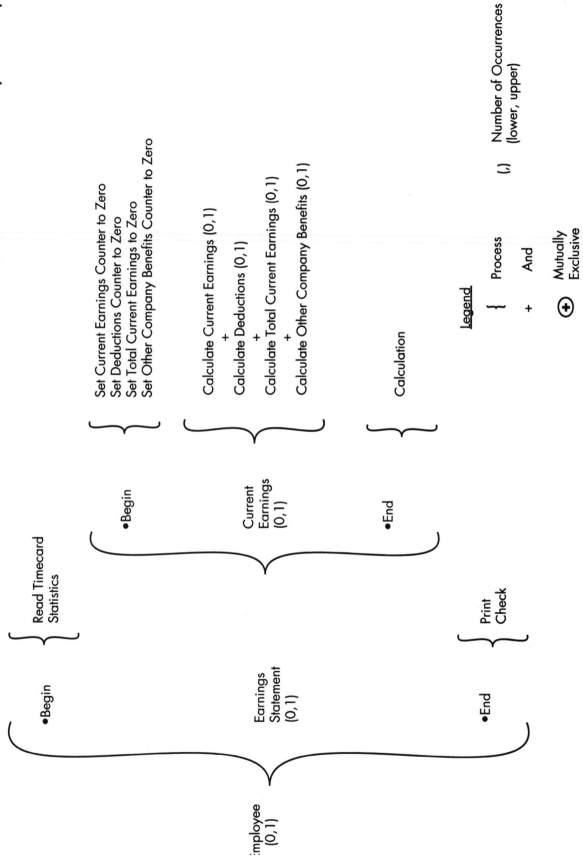

Read Timecard Statistics

Begin

Set Current Earnings Counter to Zero
Set Deductions Counter to Zero
Set Total Current Earnings to Zero
Set Other Company Benefits Counter to Zero

Current Earnings (0,1)

Calculate Current Earnings (0,1)
+
Calculate Deductions (0,1)
+
Calculate Total Current Earnings (0,1)
+
Calculate Other Company Benefits (0,1)

End

Calculation

Earnings Statement (0,1)

Print Check

Employee (0,1)

Legend

{ Process

+ And

⊕ Mutually Exclusive

(,) Number of Occurrences (lower, upper)

PROTOTYPING CHECKLIST OVERVIEW

I. DESCRIPTION

- Lists all activities and deliverables needed for developing a model of a software product

II. OBJECTIVES

- Help identify the type of prototype to build
- Ensure that the prototype addresses the minimum requirements identified by the user

III. ORGANIZATION

- Refer to Systems Analysts (1.1.1.2) in the Organization and Responsibilities Chart

IV. SCHEDULE

- Refer to the Requirements (2.0), Alternatives (3.0), Specifications (4.0), Design (5.0), and Code and Test (6.0) phases of the Software Life Cycle Chart

PROTOTYPING CHECKLIST

I. Determine type of prototype to develop, such as:
- ☐ Throwaway
- ☐ Application
- ☐ Rapid

II. Identify participants to involve, such as:
- ☐ Users
- ☐ Computing professionals, like:
  - ☐ Systems analysts
  - ☐ Application programmers
  - ☐ Systems programmers
  - ☐ Systems designers

III. Determine prototype tools, such as:
- A. Hardware, like:
  - ☐ Microcomputers
  - ☐ Terminals
  - ☐ Batch
  - ☐ Online
  - ☐ Printers, like:
    - ☐ Impact
    - ☐ Nonimpact
  - ☐ Modems
- B. Software, like:
  - ☐ High-level language
  - ☐ Screen generator
  - ☐ Report writer
  - ☐ Data dictionary
  - ☐ Database management system

IV. Select prototype techniques to employ, such as:
- ☐ Narrative descriptions
- ☐ Logical models
- ☐ Physical models

V. Address project management considerations, which include:

- ☐ Objectives
- ☐ Schedule
- ☐ Iterations
- ☐ Estimates
- ☐ Responsibilities
- ☐ Budget
- ☐ Risk assessment
- ☐ Chargeback
- ☐ Documentation

VI. Address requirements, which include:

- ☐ Inputs
- ☐ Outputs
- ☐ Functions
- ☐ Interfaces
- ☐ Databases
- ☐ Constraints
- ☐ Performance and reliability
- ☐ Screens

VII. Address design considerations, which include:

- ☐ Program design, like:
  - ☐ Logical design, like:
    - ☐ Modules
    - ☐ Module hierarchy/relationship
  - ☐ Physical design
- ☐ Database design, like:
  - ☐ Logical design
  - ☐ Physical design
- ☐ Screens, like:
  - ☐ Appearance
  - ☐ Navigation
- ☐ Reports, like:
  - ☐ Screen
  - ☐ Hardcopy

VIII. Consider demonstration details, which include:
- A. Technical, like:
  - ☐ Programs
  - ☐ Screens
  - ☐ Databases
  - ☐ Functions
  - ☐ Inputs
  - ☐ Outputs
  - ☐ Menu structure
- B. Administrative, like:
  - ☐ Participants
  - ☐ Location
  - ☐ Objectives
  - ☐ Time
  - ☐ Resources

IX. Determine refinements (additions, deletions, changes) to prototype, which include:
- ☐ Inputs
- ☐ Outputs
- ☐ Functions
- ☐ Interfaces
- ☐ Databases
- ☐ Screens

X. Address acceptance considerations, which include:
- ☐ Mode of acceptance
- ☐ Change control

REQUIREMENTS DEFINITION DOCUMENT OVERVIEW

I. DESCRIPTION

- Describes those capabilities, features, and other criteria that a software system must address

II. OBJECTIVES

- Record specifications for future reference
- Improve communication among project participants enabling effective change control
- Facilitate identification of needs that a new system must address

III. ORGANIZATION

- Refer to Systems Analysts (1.1.1.2), Configuration Management Specialists (1.2.4), and Project Manager (1.6) in the Organization and Responsibilities Chart

IV. SCHEDULE

- Refer to the Requirements (2.0), Alternatives (3.0), Specifications (4.0), Design (5.0), Code and Test (6.0), Verification/Validation (7.0), Maintenance (11.0), and Enhancements (12.0) phases of the Software Life Cycle Chart

REQUIREMENTS DEFINITION DOCUMENT

I. Present title page, which includes:
 A. Document title
 B. Document number
 C. Original release date
 D. Current release date
 E. Current revision number
 F. Appropriate signatures and date

II. Present modifications sheet, which includes:
 A. Sequentially numbered list of changes
 B. Explanation of changes
 C. Page numbers of changes
 D. Appropriate signatures and date

III. Present table of contents, which includes:
 A. Section headings
 B. Chapter titles
 C. Chapter subtitles
 D. Relevant page numbers

IV. Present executive summary, which includes:
 A. Overview
 B. Principal points

V. Present introduction, which includes:
 A. Goals
 B. Scope
 C. Objectives, like:
 • Technical
 • Business
 D. Background information

VI. Present Feasibility Study Document overview
VII. Present existing environment overview, which includes:
 A. Inputs

B. Processes

C. Outputs

D. Mission

E. Standards

F. Users

G. Documentation

VIII. Describe automated requirements, related to:

    A. Data, like:
- Data structure
- Data flow
- Dynamics
- Static (tables)
- Interfaces to other systems
- File descriptions

    B. Inputs, like:
- Screens
- Screen navigation
- Forms
- Interfaces to other systems
- Sources
- Files

    C. Outputs, like:
- Reports
- Graphical displays
- Interfaces to other systems
- Recipients
- Files

    D. Functions and processes, like:
- Critical
- Noncritical
- Logic
- Schedule

    E. Physical, like:
- Hardware
- Software
- Documentation

IX. Describe manual requirements, related to:
   A. Data, like:
      - Data flow
      - Forms
      - Data structure
      - Narrative descriptions
      - Data collection
   B. Inputs
   C. Functions
   D. Outputs, like:
      - Reports
      - Graphical display

X. Describe special requirements, related to:
   A. Organizational structure
   B. Documentation
   C. Facilities
   D. Supplies
   E. Approvals
   F. Performance, like:
      - Throughput
      - Volume
      - Frequency
      - Threshold
      - Response time
   G. Personnel
   H. Security/privacy

XI. Describe additional requirements

XII. Prepare glossary

XIII. Attach appendixes

Chapter 3

Alternatives

ALTERNATIVES ANALYSIS DOCUMENT OVERVIEW

I. DESCRIPTION

- Describes the various alternatives that a computing solution can take and provides a recommendation on which alternative to pursue

II. OBJECTIVES

- Provide an objective way to select an appropriate computing alternative
- Document the various alternatives for future reference

III. ORGANIZATION

- Refer to Systems Analysts (1.1.1.2), Configuration Management Specialists (1.2.4), and Project Manager (1.6) in the Organization and Responsibilities Chart

IV. SCHEDULE

- Refer to the Alternatives Phase (3.0) of the Software Life Cycle Chart

ALTERNATIVES ANALYSIS DOCUMENT

I. Present title page, which includes:
    A. Document title
    B. Document number
    C. Original release date
    D. Current release date
    E. Current revision number
    F. Appropriate signatures and date

II. Present modifications sheet, which includes:
    A. Sequentially numbered list of changes
    B. Explanation of changes
    C. Page numbers of changes
    D. Appropriate signatures and date

III. Present table of contents, which includes:
    A. Section headings
    B. Chapter titles
    C. Chapter subtitles
    D. Relevant page numbers

IV. Present executive summary, which includes:
    A. Overview
    B. Principal points

V. Present introduction, which includes:
    A. Goals
    B. Scope
    C. Objectives, like:
        • Technical
        • Business
    D. Background information

VI. Present Requirements Definition Document overview, which includes:
   A. Inputs
   B. Outputs
   C. Functions
   D. Interfaces
   E. Storage
   F. Retrieval

VII. Describe evaluation criteria, which include:
   A. System goals and objectives
   B. Critical requirements, like:
      • Inputs
      • Outputs
      • Functions
      • Interfaces
      • Storage
      • Retrieval

VIII. For each possible solution, prepare:
   A. Description, which includes:
      • Functions
      • Data structure
      • Operational features
      • Technical features
      • File descriptions
   B. Advantages, which include:
      • Technical advantages
      • Operational advantages
      • Financial advantages
      • Intangible/nonquantifiable advantages
   C. Disadvantages, which include:
      • Technical disadvantages
      • Operational disadvantages
      • Financial disadvantages
      • Intangible/nonquantifiable advantages
   D. Ranking

IX. Make recommendations, which include:
   A. Selection
   B. Rationale

X. Prepare glossary

XI. Attach appendixes

Chapter 4

Specifications

FUNCTIONAL SPECIFICATIONS DOCUMENT OVERVIEW

I. DESCRIPTION

- Describes how the system will appear to the user (for example, the appearance of screens, movement from screen to screen, the structure of data, error messages, etc.) and the design of the system

II. OBJECTIVES

- Record how the system should appear to the user, thereby enabling change control
- Reduce communication problems between the user and the developer
- Provide useful reference material during the Design Phase and Sustaining operations
- Give technical writers information to start developing User Manual

III. ORGANIZATION

- Refer to Database Analysts (1.1.1.1), Systems Analysts (1.1.1.2), Systems Designers (1.1.2.1), Configuration Management Specialists (1.2.4), and Project Manager (1.6) in the Organization and Responsibilities Chart

IV. SCHEDULE

- Refer to the Design (5.0) and Code and Test (6.0) phases of the Software Life Cycle Chart

FUNCTIONAL SPECIFICATIONS DOCUMENT

I. Present title page, which includes:
   - A. Document title
   - B. Document number
   - C. Original release date
   - D. Current release date
   - E. Current revision number
   - F. Appropriate signatures and date

II. Present modifications sheet, which includes:
   - A. Sequentially numbered list of changes
   - B. Explanation of changes
   - C. Page numbers of changes
   - D. Appropriate signatures and date

III. Present table of contents, which includes:
   - A. Section headings
   - B. Chapter titles
   - C. Chapter subtitles
   - D. Relevant page numbers

IV. Present executive summary, which includes:
   - A. Overview
   - B. Principal points

V. Present introduction, which includes:
   - A. Goals
   - B. Scope
   - C. Objectives, like:
      - Technical
      - Business
   - D. Background information

VI. Present requirements definition overview, which includes:
   - A. Inputs
   - B. Outputs

C. Functions
D. Interfaces
E. Storage
F. Retrieval
G. Special considerations

VII. Present alternatives analysis overview, which includes:
   A. Alternatives, which include:
      • Inputs
      • Outputs
      • Functions
      • Interfaces
      • Storage
      • Retrieval
      • Costs
      • Schedule
      • File descriptions
      • Special considerations, assumptions, and constraints
   B. Recommendations

VIII. Present detail specifications, which include:
   A. Functions
   B. Inputs, like:
      • Media
      • Format
   C. Outputs, like:
      • Reports
   D. Screens, like:
      • Format
      • Content
      • Navigation
   E. Data structure, like:
      • Tables
      • Files
      • Format
      • Records
   F. Interfaces
   G. Equipment, like:
      • Central processing unit (CPU)
      • Storage

- Input/output (I/O) devices
- Data communication

H. Software, like:
- Systems
- Application

I. Security, like:
- General controls
- Input controls
- Processing controls
- Output controls

J. Performance considerations, like:
- Throughput
- Timing
- Volume
- Accuracy

K. Environmental considerations

L. Documentation

M. Restart and recovery, like:
- Hardware
- Software
- Data

N. Manual

IX. Describe impact analysis, which includes:
A. Technical impacts, like:
- Hardware
- Software
- Data

B. Operational impacts, like:
- Personnel
- Procedures
- Organizational

C. Financial impacts, like:
- Recurring
- Nonrecurring

X. Prepare glossary

XI. Attach appendixes

SYSTEM/SUBSYSTEM SPECIFICATIONS CHECKLIST OVERVIEW

I. DESCRIPTION

- Provide list of design, test, and performance activities

II. OBJECTIVES

- Identify functions and ensure that they perform as defined
- Identify interfaces and ensure that they perform as designed

III. ORGANIZATION

- Refer to Supervisor of Analysis (1.1.1) and Systems Designers (1.1.2.1) in the Organization and Responsibilities Chart

IV. SCHEDULE

- Refer to the Specifications phase (4.0) of the Software Life Cycle Chart

SYSTEM/SUBSYSTEM SPECIFICATIONS CHECKLIST

I. Identify and document system/subsystem design specifications, including:
- [ ] System functionalities
- [ ] Subsystem functionalities
- [ ] System design
- [ ] Subsystem design
- [ ] Physical flow
- [ ] Logical flow
- [ ] Interfaces
- [ ] Standards

II. Identify and document system/subsystem test specifications, including:
- [ ] System tests
- [ ] Subsystem tests
- [ ] System and subsystem environment compatibility

III. Address system/subsystem performance, including:
- [ ] Maintainability
- [ ] Reliability
- [ ] Safety
- [ ] Quality

IV. Address other system/subsystem areas for review, including:
- [ ] Staff allocations and assignments
- [ ] Training requirements
- [ ] Identification and order of equipment
- [ ] Identification and order of special items

DATABASE SPECIFICATIONS DOCUMENT OVERVIEW

I. DESCRIPTION

- Establish procedures and processes for database design and support
- Provide plans for environments, testing, and backup and recovery
- When performing database design work, an off-the-shelf software package is recommended over paper and pencil to reduce labor intensiveness

II. OBJECTIVE

- Identify and document database(s) including installation, flow, and maintenance

III. ORGANIZATION

- Refer to Manager of Development (1.1), Supervisor of Analysis (1.1.1, 1.4.1), Database Analysts (1.1.1.1, 1.4.1.1), Manager of Technical Support (1.2), Database Administrators (1.2.3), Configuration Management Specialists (1.2.4), and Project Manager (1.6) in the Organization and Responsibilities Chart

IV. SCHEDULE

- Refer to the Specifications (4.0), Design (5.0), and Code and Test (6.0) phases of the Software Life Cycle Chart

DATABASE SPECIFICATIONS DOCUMENT

    I. Present title page, which includes:
- A. Document title
- B. Document number
- C. Original release date
- D. Current release date
- E. Current revision number
- F. Appropriate signatures and date

   II. Present modifications sheet, which includes:
- A. Sequentially numbered list of changes
- B. Explanation of changes
- C. Page numbers of changes
- D. Appropriate signatures and date

  III. Present table of contents, which includes:
- A. Section headings
- B. Chapter titles
- C. Chapter subtitles
- D. Relevant page numbers

  IV. Present executive summary, which includes:
- A. Overview
- B. Principal features

   V. Present introduction, which includes:
- A. Scope
- B. Background information

  VI. Define and develop database specifications, which include:
- A. Design
- B. Support
- C. Schemas
- D. Physical database environments
- E. Database test plans
- F. Backup and recovery plan

G. Database management system software
H. Access security protection
I. Data relationships and usage enforcement
J. Database conversions
K. Performance monitoring and reporting
L. Database application programs
M. Database application programs testing
N. Standardized naming conventions
O. Interface with other systems
P. Coordinate audit checks

VII. Prepare glossary

VIII. Attach appendixes

RECORD LAYOUT FORM OVERVIEW

I. DESCRIPTION

- Describes the characteristics of a record that make up particular file fields of which the file is composed

II. OBJECTIVES

- Document the layout for future reference
- Improve communication among project participants
- Enable effective change control

III. ORGANIZATION

- Refer to Database Analysts (1.1.1.1), Systems Analysts (1.1.1.2), Systems Programmers (1.1.3.1, 1.4.2.1), Application Programmers (1.1.3.2, 1.4.2.2), and Project Manager (1.6) in the Organization and Responsibilities Chart

IV. SCHEDULE

- Refer to the Requirements (2.0), Design (5.0), Code and Test (6.0), Maintenance (11.0), and Enhancements (12.0) phases of the Software Life Cycle Chart

RECORD LAYOUT FORM

FIELD	DESCRIPTION	NO. OF CHARACTERS	SOURCE	COMMENTS
LN	Last Name	15	File XB01	Alpha
FN	First Name	10	File XB01	Alpha
MI	Middle Initial	2	File XB01	Alpha
ADD	Address	25	File CD03	Alphanumeric

RECORD LAYOUT FORM

FIELD	DESCRIPTION	NO. OF CHARACTERS	SOURCE	COMMENTS

FILE DESCRIPTION FORM OVERVIEW

I. DESCRIPTION

- Shows the composition of a file, its format, and its structure

II. OBJECTIVES

- Document the makeup of a file so that application and systems programmers can refer to it when modifying or building programs
- Reduce communication problems
- Help build compatibility among systems

III. ORGANIZATION

- Refer to Systems Analysts (1.1.1.2, 1.4.1.2), Systems Programmers (1.1.3.1, 1.4.2.1), Application Programmers (1.1.3.2, 1.4.2.2), and Project Manager (1.6) in the Organization and Responsibilities Chart

IV. SCHEDULE

- Refer to the Requirements (2.0), Design (5.0), Code and Test (6.0), Maintenance (11.0), and Enhancements (12.0) phases of the Software Life Cycle Chart

FILE DESCRIPTION FORM

FILE NAME
Employee Name

FILE NUMBER
XB01

CREATION DATE
5/17/9X

LAST REVISION
2/27/9X

FILE SIZE
100,000 bytes

LOGICAL RECORD LENGTH
150

BLOCKING FACTOR
1500

RECORD TYPE
FB

AFFECTED PROGRAMS
All Payroll Programs

FILE DESCRIPTION FORM

FILE NAME   FILE NUMBER   CREATION DATE

LAST REVISION   FILE SIZE   LOGICAL RECORD LENGTH

BLOCKING FACTOR   RECORD TYPE   AFFECTED PROGRAMS

SOFTWARE ERGONOMICS CHECKLIST OVERVIEW

I. DESCRIPTION

- List of characteristics to incorporate in software during its construction
- Emphasizes the interaction between the software and the user
- Emphasizes user interaction over technical capabilities

II. OBJECTIVES

- Help ensure that newly developed software accounts for ergonomic features
- Facilitate greater usage of software in the future
- Help reduce user frustration with software

III. ORGANIZATION

- Refer to Systems Analysts (1.1.1.2) and Testers (1.2.7) in the Organization and Responsibilities Chart

IV. SCHEDULE

- Refer to the Requirements (2.0), Specifications (4.0), and Verification/Validation (7.0) phases of the Software Life Cycle Chart

SOFTWARE ERGONOMICS CHECKLIST

I. Define screen characteristics regarding:

☐ Color, like:
    ☐ Consistency

    ☐ Usage
☐ Organization, like:
    ☐ Arrangement

    ☐ Consistency
☐ Movement from field to field, like:
    ☐ Autoskip

    ☐ Tabbing
☐ Fields, like:
    ☐ Content

    ☐ Captions

    ☐ Size
☐ Components, like:
    ☐ Titles

    ☐ Character size
☐ Comprehension, like:
    ☐ Clear

    ☐ Concise

    ☐ Jargon-free

II. Address screen navigation features regarding:

    ☐ Structure

    ☐ Order

III. Define usage regarding:

☐ Performance, like:
    ☐ Flexibility

    ☐ Complexity

    ☐ Response time

    ☐ Consistency

    ☐ Information handling

- [ ] Edits, like:
  - [ ] Additions
  - [ ] Deletions
  - [ ] Changes
  - [ ] Defaults
- [ ] Error handling actions
- [ ] Recovery actions

Chapter 5

Design

STRUCTURE CHART OVERVIEW

I. DESCRIPTION

- Illustrates the modular structure of a system, specifically software, and the relationship of those modules to one another

II. OBJECTIVES

- Visually show the structure of software in a computing system
- Document that structure for future reference
- Improve communication between designers and programmers
- Help reduce the complexity of software
- Lead to good configuration control of software

III. ORGANIZATION

- Refer to Systems Designers (1.1.2.1), Systems Programmers (1.1.3.1), Application Programmers (1.1.3.2), Configuration Management Specialists (1.2.4), and Project Manager (1.6) in the Organization and Responsibilities Chart

IV. SCHEDULE

- Refer to the Design (5.0), Code and Test (6.0), Maintenance (11.0), and Enhancements (12.0) phases of the Software Life Cycle Chart

STRUCTURE CHART

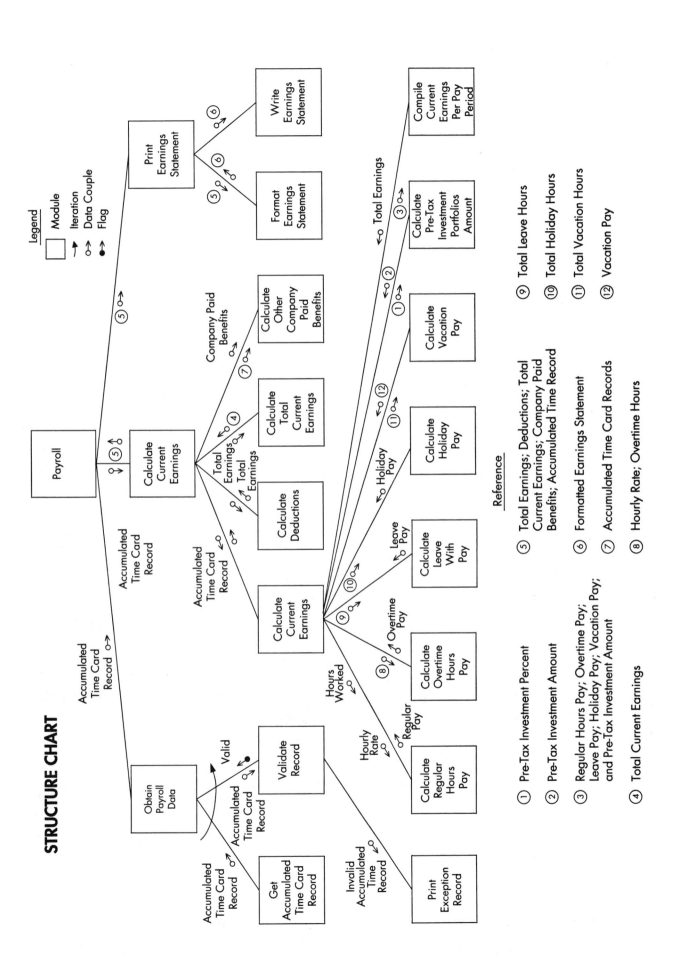

Legend

☐ Module
→ Iteration
○→ Data Couple
●→ Flag

Reference

① Pre-Tax Investment Percent
② Pre-Tax Investment Amount
③ Regular Hours Pay; Overtime Pay; Leave Pay; Holiday Pay; Vacation Pay; and Pre-Tax Investment Amount
④ Total Current Earnings
⑤ Total Earnings; Deductions; Total Current Earnings; Company Paid Benefits; Accumulated Time Record
⑥ Formatted Earnings Statement
⑦ Accumulated Time Card Records
⑧ Hourly Rate; Overtime Hours
⑨ Total Leave Hours
⑩ Total Holiday Hours
⑪ Total Vacation Hours
⑫ Vacation Pay

STRUCTURE CHART CHECKLIST

I. Determine the contents of the structure chart, including:
- ☐ Modules
- ☐ Data couples
- ☐ Flag couples
- ☐ Hierarchy of modules
- ☐ Number of levels

II. Determine the following for each module:
- ☐ Input
- ☐ Output
- ☐ Descriptor
- ☐ Position with structure
- ☐ Function

NASSI–SHNEIDERMAN CHARTS OVERVIEW

I. DESCRIPTION

- Displays visually the steps and logical sequence of those steps to incorporate in a program
- Often drawn as a substitute for a flowchart; however, some programmers build them to complement the flowchart

II. OBJECTIVES

- Help comprehension of programs
- Improve the modularity of programs
- Facilitate communication
- Provide useful documentation for development and maintenance programmers

III. ORGANIZATION

- Refer to Systems Programmers (1.1.3.1, 1.4.2.1), Application Programmers (1.1.3.2, 1.4.2.2), and Project Manager (1.6) in the Organization and Responsibilities Chart

IV. SCHEDULE

- Refer to the Code and Test (6.0), Maintenance (11.0), and Enhancements (12.0) phases of the Software Life Cycle Chart

NASSI–SHNEIDERMAN CHART
(SEQUENCE)

CALCULATE GROSS PAY	FUNCTION
CALCULATE TAXES	FUNCTION
CALCULATE NET PAY	FUNCTION

NASSI–SHNEIDERMAN CHART
(DECISION)

DECISION

OVERTIME PAY?	
YES	NO
CALCULATE TIME-AND-A-HALF PAY	CALCULATE GROSS PAY
CALCULATE DOUBLE-TIME PAY	
SUM OVERTIME PAY	
CALCULATE GROSS PAY	

FUNCTION

NASSI–SHNEIDERMAN CHART
(ITERATION)

FUNCTION

CALCULATE LOCAL TAXES	
CALCULATE STATE TAXES	
CALCULATE FEDERAL TAXES	
CALCULATE TAXES UNTIL TAXES = 50% OF GROSS PAY	

ITERATION

NASSI–SHNEIDERMAN CHART
(COMBINATION)

DECISION

OVERTIME PAY?	
YES	NO

ACTION

CALCULATE TIME-AND-A-HALF PAY	CALCULATE GROSS PAY
CALCULATE DOUBLE-TIME PAY	
SUM OVERTIME PAY	
CALCULATE GROSS PAY	

CALCULATE LOCAL TAXES
CALCULATE STATE TAXES
CALCULATE FEDERAL TAXES

CALCULATE TAXES UNTIL TAXES = 50% OF GROSS PAY

CALCULATE NET PAY

ITERATION

NASSI–SHNEIDERMAN CHARTS CHECKLIST

I. Identify control structures, including:
  - ☐ Sequence
  - ☐ Decision
  - ☐ Iteration
  - ☐ Combination

II Determine descriptors for each diagram, including:
  - ☐ Command verb
  - ☐ Object

PROGRAM FLOWCHART OVERVIEW

I. DESCRIPTION

- Illustrates the logical constructs included in a software program

II. OBJECTIVES

- Display the logical sequence of steps that occurs in a program
- Improve communication among programmers
- Create reference material on what a program does

III. ORGANIZATION

- Refer to Application Programmers (1.1.3.2, 1.4.2.2), Systems Analysts (1.4.1.2), and Project Manager (1.6) in the Organization and Responsibilities Chart

IV. SCHEDULE

- Refer to the Code and Test (6.0), Maintenance (11.0), and Enhancements (12.0) phases of the Software Life Cycle Chart

PROGRAM FLOWCHART CHECKLIST

I. Identify the symbols to use, including:
- ☐ Start and termination
- ☐ Input and output
- ☐ Process
- ☐ Decision
- ☐ Subroutine

II. Determine descriptors for each symbol:
- ☐ Command verb
- ☐ Object

PROGRAM FLOWCHART

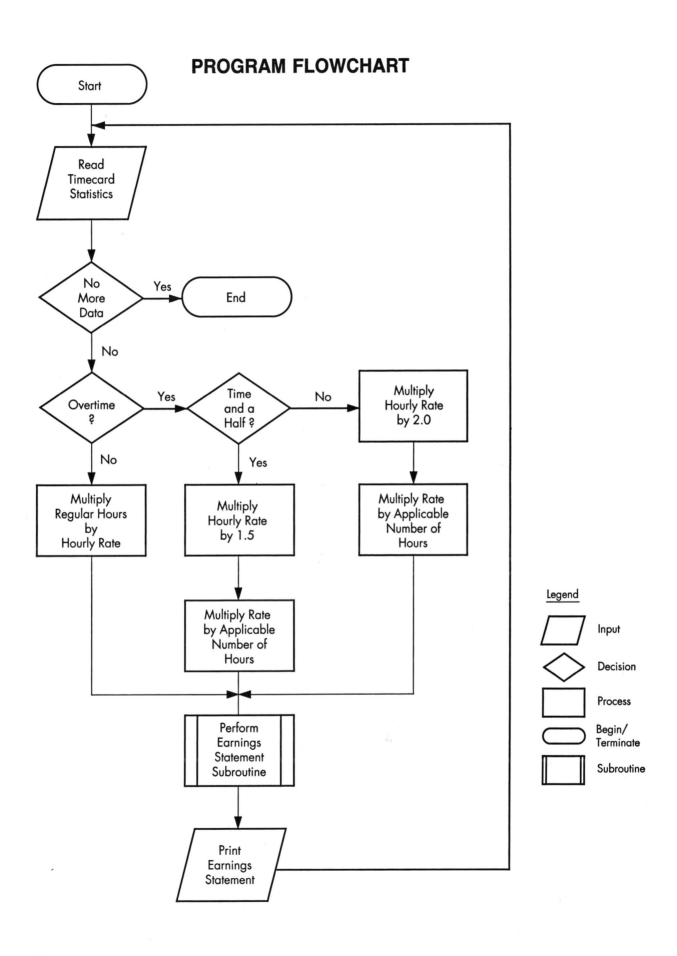

SYSTEMS FLOWCHART OVERVIEW

I. DESCRIPTION

- Shows the manual and automated activities that occur within a system and its major components

II. OBJECTIVES

- Display activities and components of a system
- Improve communication by providing an overall picture of a system
- Provide useful documentation for reference

III. ORGANIZATION

- Refer to Systems Analysts (1.1.1.2), Systems Programmers (1.1.3.1), Application Programmers (1.1.3.2), Job Schedulers (1.3.2.1), and Project Manager (1.6) in the Organization and Responsibilities Chart

IV. SCHEDULE

- Refer to the Alternatives (3.0), Design (5.0), Code and Test (6.0), Maintenance (11.0), and Enhancements (12.0) phases of the Software Life Cycle Chart

SYSTEMS FLOWCHART CHECKLIST

I. Identify the symbols to use, including:
- ☐ Merge
- ☐ Manual operation
- ☐ Document
- ☐ Magnetic drum
- ☐ Tape
- ☐ Disk pack
- ☐ Display
- ☐ Punched card
- ☐ Online storage

II. Determine descriptors for each symbol, including:
- ☐ Command verb
- ☐ Object

SYSTEMS FLOWCHART

Payroll Update Form → Local Payroll Dept. Reviews Form → Key in Data → Validate Data → Record on Transaction File → A

Master File Copy → Validate Data

Validate Data → Exception Report

Record on Transaction File → Transaction File

A → Print Pay Transaction Record → Print Transaction Record → Send Pay Transaction Record to Employee

Print Pay Transaction Record → Update Master File in Evening

Transaction File → Update Master File in Evening

Update Master File in Evening → New Master File Copy

Master File Copy → Update Master File in Evening

New Master File Copy → Transmit Copy of New Master File to Home Office → Company Payroll Database

Legend

Document	
Manual Operation	
Magnetic Tape	
Process	
Magnetic Storage	

REPORT LAYOUT FORM OVERVIEW

I. DESCRIPTION

- Displays how reports should appear when printed on paper

II. OBJECTIVES

- Improve communication
- Preclude repetition of tasks
- Help prevent the overlooking of requirements
- Provide documentation

III. ORGANIZATION

- Refer to Systems Analysts (1.1.1.2), Application Programmers (1.1.3.2, 1.4.2.2), and Project Manager (1.6) in the Organization and Responsibilities Chart

IV. SCHEDULE

- Refer to the Requirements (2.0), Maintenance (11.0), and Enhancements (12.0) phases of the Software Life Cycle Chart

REPORT LAYOUT FORM

XX/XX/XX

EMPLOYEE CURRENT EARNINGS REPORT

PAGE XXX

EMPLOYEE NUMBER	EMPLOYEE NAME	REGULAR HOURS	OVERTIME HOURS	HOURLY RATE	CURRENT EARNINGS
XXXXX	XXXXXXXXXXXXXXXXXXXXXXX	XXX	XXX	XX.XX	XXXXX.XX

DATABASE DESIGN FLOWCHARTS OVERVIEW

I. DESCRIPTION

- Displays the logical structure of the database using three common forms of database structures, which are hierarchical, network, and relational

II. OBJECTIVES

- Document the logical structure of the database
- Improve communications and understanding among project team members

III. ORGANIZATION

- Refer to Database Analysts (1.1.1.1, 1.4.1.1), Database Administrators (1.2.3), Configuration Management Specialists (1.2.4), and Project Manager (1.6) in the Organization and Responsibilities Chart

IV. SCHEDULE

- Refer to the Specifications (4.0) and Design (5.0) phases of the Software Life Cycle Chart

DATABASE DESIGN CHECKLIST

I. Identify the type of database to design, such as:
- ☐ Hierarchical
- ☐ Network
- ☐ Relation

II. For each database schema, determine:
- ☐ Elements
- ☐ Relationship among elements
- ☐ Characteristics of each element, like:
    - ☐ Descriptor
    - ☐ Composition

HIERARCHICAL DATABASE DESIGN

```
                                              Name
                                               |
        ┌──────────┬──────────────┬────────────┼──────────────┐
        │          │              │            │              │
  Social        Date of        Home        Date of         Gross
  Security      Birth          Address      Hire            Pay
  Number                                                     │
                                              ┌──────────────┼──────────────┐
                                              │              │              │
                                        Cumulative      Regular Pay    Overtime Pay
                                        Hours           Rate           Rate
                                              │
                                    ┌─────────┴─────────┐
                                    │                   │
                                Regular             Overtime
                                Hours               Hours
```

HIERARCHICAL DATABASE DESIGN

01	NAME		
	03	LASTNAME	PIC X(25)
	03	FIRSTNAME	PIC X(20)
	03	MIDDLENAME	PIC X(20)
01	SOCIAL SECURITY NUMBER		
	03	SSN	PIC X(11)
01	DATE OF HIRE		
	03	DOH	PIC X(8)
01	DATE OF BIRTH		
	03	DOB	PIC X(8)
01	HOME ADDRESS		
	03	RESIDENCE	PIC X(30)
01	GROSS PAY		
	03	PAY	PIC X(8)
01	CUMULATIVE HOURS		
	03	TOTAL HOURS	PIC X(5)
01	OVERTIME HOURS		
	03	TIME-AND-A-HALF HOURS	PIC X(5)
	03	DOUBLE-TIME HOURS	PIC X(5)
01	REGULAR HOURS		
	03	NORMAL HOURS	PIC X(5)
01	REGULAR PAY RATE		
	03	HOURLY RATE	PIC X(6)
01	OVERTIME PAY RATE		
	03	TIME-AND-A-HALF RATE	PIC X(6)
	03	DOUBLE-TIME RATE	PIC X(6)

NETWORK DATABASE DESIGN

RELATIONAL DATABASE DESIGN

Employee Table

Employee Number	Name	Organization	Social Security Number
1111	Smith, John	Finance	145-46-5452

Timecard Table

Social Security Number	Employee Number	Name	Organization	Regular Hours	Overtime (Time and a Half)	Overtime (Double Time)	Date Received	Date Verified
145-46-5452	1111	Smith, John	Finance	80	10	5	2/2/XX	2/2/XX

Employee Table

Control Number	Date Received	Approved By	Date Entered Into Computer
0817	2/5/XX	Wilson, Pete	2/6/XX

Employee Table

Social Security Number	Date Received	Assigned Control Number	Approved By	Date Submitted to Payroll
145-46-5452	2/3/XX	0817	Jones, Rod	2/4/XX

PRELIMINARY DESIGN DOCUMENT OVERVIEW

I. DESCRIPTION

- Describes the logical and physical design of a system that will be constructed during the detail design phase of a project

II. OBJECTIVES

- Document logical and physical designs
- Improve communication between system designers and programmers
- Provide a basis for configuration management and change control

III. ORGANIZATION

- Refer to Systems Designers (1.1.2.1), Configuration Management Specialists (1.2.4), and Project Manager (1.6) in the Organization and Responsibilities Chart

IV. SCHEDULE

- Refer to the Design (5.0), Code and Test (6.0), Maintenance (11.0), and Enhancements (12.0) phases of the Software Life Cycle Chart

PRELIMINARY DESIGN DOCUMENT

  I. Present title page, which includes:
- A. Document title
- B. Document number
- C. Original release date
- D. Current release date
- E. Current revision number
- F. Appropriate signatures and date

  II. Present modifications sheet, which includes:
- A. Sequentially numbered list of changes
- B. Explanation of changes
- C. Page numbers of changes
- D. Appropriate signatures and date

  III. Present table of contents, which includes:
- A. Section headings
- B. Chapter titles
- C. Chapter subtitles
- D. Relevant page numbers

  IV. Present executive summary, which includes:
- A. Overview
- B. Principal points

  V. Present introduction, which includes:
- A. Goals
- B. Scope
- C. Objectives, like:
  - Technical
  - Business
- D. Background information

  VI. Present requirements definition overview, which includes:
- A. Existing environment description, like:
  - Logical requirements

- Physical requirements
- B. Special considerations, constraints, and limitations

VII. Present alternatives analysis overview, which includes:
- A. For each alternative:
  - Description
  - Advantages
  - Disadvantages
- B. Recommendations

VIII. Present functional specifications overview, which includes:
- A. Technical considerations
- B. Operational considerations
- C. Impacts

IX. Present design, which includes:
- A. Module description, like:
  - Name
  - Function
  - Inputs
  - Logic
  - Outputs
- B. Configuration and logic of modules
- C. Data description, like:
  - Structure
  - Inputs
  - Outputs
  - Static data
  - Dynamic data (input and output)
- D. Security description, like:
  - General controls
  - Input controls
  - Processing controls
  - Output controls
- E. Software description, like:
  - Application software
  - Operating system
- F. Performance description, like:
  - Response time

- Throughput
- Volume
- Interfaces

G. Hardware description
H. Programs description
I. Storage description
J. Ergonomic

X. Describe design implementation, which includes:
A. Alternative physical design descriptions, which cover:
- Manual features and capabilities
- Automated features and capabilities
- Schedule
- Cost
- Resources

B. Design comparison, which covers:
- Evaluation criteria
- Recommendation

XI. Prepare glossary

XII. Attach appendixes

Chapter 6

Code and Test

DETAIL DESIGN DOCUMENT OVERVIEW

I. DESCRIPTION

- Describes the exact specifications of the program and data that will be incorporated in the new computing system

II. OBJECTIVES

- Record program and data specifications for future reference
- Improve communication among project participants
- Enable effective change control
- Facilitate the actual development of the code

III. ORGANIZATION

- Refer to Database Analysts (1.1.1.1), Systems Programmers (1.1.3.1, 1.4.2.1), Application Programmers (1.1.3.2, 1.4.2.2), Configuration Management Specialists (1.2.4), and Project Manager (1.6) in the Organization and Responsibilities Chart

IV. SCHEDULE

- Refer to the Code and Test (6.0), Maintenance (11.0), and Enhancements (12.0) phases of the Software Life Cycle Chart

DETAIL DESIGN DOCUMENT

I. Present title page, which includes:
  A. Document title
  B. Document number
  C. Original release date
  D. Current release date
  E. Current revision number
  F. Appropriate signatures and date

II. Present modifications sheet, which includes:
  A. Sequentially numbered list of changes
  B. Explanation of changes
  C. Page numbers of changes
  D. Appropriate signatures and date

III. Present table of contents, which includes:
  A. Section headings
  B. Chapter titles
  C. Chapter subtitles
  D. Relevant page numbers

IV. Present executive summary, which includes:
  A. Overview
  B. Principal points

V. Present introduction, which includes:
  A. Goals
  B. Scope
  C. Objectives, like:
    • Technical
    • Business
  D. Background information

VI. Present requirements definition overview, which includes:
  A. Existing environment description, like:
    • Logical requirements

- Physical requirements

    B. Special considerations, constraints, and limitations

VII. Present alternatives analysis overview, which includes for each alternative:
- Description
- Advantages
- Disadvantages

VIII. Present functional specifications overview, which includes:
    A. Technical considerations
    B. Operational considerations
    C. Impacts

IX. Present preliminary design overview, which includes:
    A. Design description
    B. Evaluation configuration criteria

X. Describe program design, which includes:
    A. Inputs, like:
- Description
- Format

    B. Outputs, like:
- Description
- Format

    C. Processing/functions
    D. Interfaces
    E. Data files and databases, like:
- Logical considerations
- Physical considerations

    F. Structure
    G. Performance criteria, like:
- Response time
- Throughput
- Transmission time
- Volume

    H. Logic
    I. Security/privacy
    J. Documentation, like:

- Record layouts
- File layouts
- Flowcharts
- Input–Process–Output charts

    K. Name

    L. Function/purpose

XI. Describe operating environment, which includes:

    A. Support software

    B. Equipment

    C. Storage devices

XII. Describe testing, which includes:

    A. Test data

    B. Unit testing techniques

XIII. Prepare glossary

XIV. Attach appendixes

DECISION TABLE OVERVIEW

I. DESCRIPTION

- Shows the conditions that can occur, the possible combinations thereof
- Shows the action or actions to take in response to those conditions
- Often developed in place of a Decision Tree and can accompany a complete set of Data Flow Diagrams

II. OBJECTIVES

- Simplify the way conditions and associated actions are displayed (as opposed to narrative text)
- Serve as reference material for programmers during development and sustaining activities

III. ORGANIZATION

- Refer to Systems Analysts (1.1.1.2), Systems Designers (1.1.2.1), Systems Programmers (1.1.3.1), Application Programmers (1.1.3.2), and Project Manager (1.6) in the Organization and Responsibilities Chart

IV. SCHEDULE

- Refer to the Requirements (2.0), Alternatives (3.0), Design (5.0), Code and Test (6.0), Verification/Validation (7.0), Maintenance (11.0), and Enhancements (12.0) phases of the Software Life Cycle Chart

DECISION TABLE CHECKLIST

I. Identify the components of the decision table, including:
- ☐ Condition stub
- ☐ Action stub
- ☐ Rules

II. Determine the contents for:
- ☐ Condition stub
- ☐ Action stub
- ☐ Rules

DECISION TABLE

		RULES			
	1	2	3	4	5
CONDITIONS					
1. WORK LESS THAN 40 HOURS	YES	NO	NO	NO	NO
2. WORK 40 HOURS	NO	YES	NO	NO	NO
3. WORK MORE THAN 40 HOURS BUT LESS THAN 50 HOURS	NO	NO	YES	NO	NO
4. WORK 50 HOURS OR MORE BUT NOT ON WEEKENDS	NO	NO	NO	YES	NO
5. WORK 50 HOURS OR MORE PLUS WEEKENDS	NO	NO	NO	NO	YES
ACTIONS					
1. PAY REGULAR RATE	X	X			
2. PAY REGULAR PLUS TIME AND A HALF			X	X	
3. PAY REGULAR PLUS TIME AND A HALF AND DOUBLE TIME					X

CONDITION STUB

ACTION STUB

DECISION TREE OVERVIEW

I. DESCRIPTION

- Shows the conditions that can occur, the possible combinations thereof
- Shows the action or actions to take in response to those conditions
- Often developed in place of a Decision Table and can accompany a complete set of Data Flow Diagrams

II. OBJECTIVES

- Simplify the way conditions and associated actions are displayed (as opposed to narrative text)
- Serve as reference material for programmers during development and sustaining activities

III. ORGANIZATION

- Refer to Systems Analysts (1.1.1.2), Systems Designers (1.1.2.1.), Application Programmers (1.1.3.2), and Project Manager (1.6) in the Organization and Responsibilities Chart

IV. SCHEDULE

- Refer to the Requirements (2.0), Alternatives (3.0), Design (5.0), Code and Test (6.0), Validation/Verification (7.0), Maintenance (11.0), and Enhancements (12.0) phases of the Software Life Cycle Chart

DECISION TREE CHECKLIST

I. **Identify the contents of the tree, including:**

☐ Conditions
☐ Actions

DECISION TREE

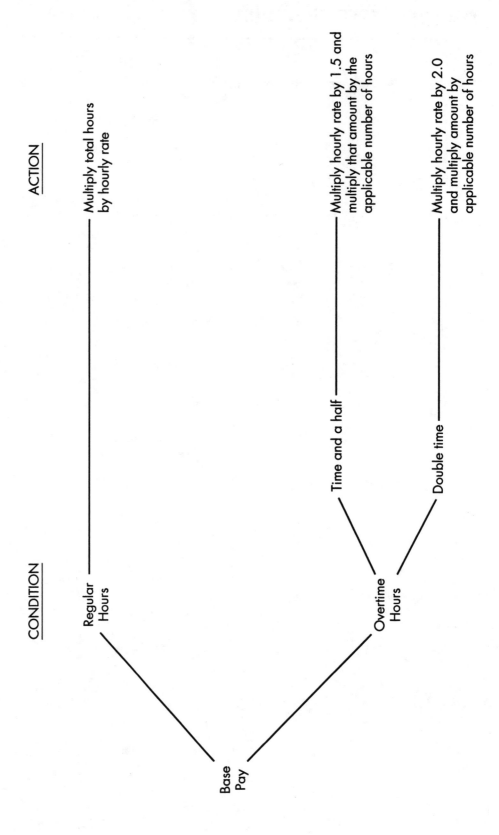

CONDITION

ACTION

Regular Hours — Multiply total hours by hourly rate

Base Pay

Overtime Hours

Time and a half — Multiply hourly rate by 1.5 and multiply that amount by the applicable number of hours

Double time — Multiply hourly rate by 2.0 and multiply amount by applicable number of hours

TEST PLAN OVERVIEW

I. DESCRIPTION

- Describes details on planning a test of a new or revised computing system
- Describes test of a new or revised computing system along with the techniques used and the expected results of the test

II. OBJECTIVES

- Increase efficiency and the effectiveness of a test
- Coordinate testing activities
- Reduce delays in testing by ensuring that the right testing resources are available at the right time

III. ORGANIZATION

- Refer to Systems Analysts (1.1.1.2), Configuration Management Specialists (1.2.4), Quality-Assurance Specialists (1.2.5), Testers (1.2.7), and Project Manager (1.6) in the Organization and Responsibilities Chart

IV. SCHEDULE

- Refer to the Requirements (2.0), Alternatives (3.0), Specifications (4.0), Design (5.0), Code and Test (6.0), and Verification/Validation (7.0) phases of the Software Life Cycle Chart

TEST PLAN

    I. Present title page, which includes:
        A. Document title
        B. Document number
        C. Original release date
        D. Current release date
        E. Current revision number
        F. Appropriate signatures and date

   II. Present modifications sheet, which includes:
        A. Sequentially numbered list of changes
        B. Explanation of changes
        C. Page numbers of changes
        D. Appropriate signatures and date

  III. Present table of contents, which includes:
        A. Section headings
        B. Chapter titles
        C. Chapter subtitles
        D. Relevant page numbers

  IV. Present executive summary, which includes:
        A. Overview
        B. Principal points

    V. Present introduction, which includes:
        A. Goals
        B. Scope
        C. Objectives, like:
            • Technical
            • Business
        D. Background information

  VI. Present system overview, which includes:
        A. Inputs

B. Outputs

C. Processes and functions

D. Interfaces

E. Data structures and relationships

F. Security

G. Limitations and constraints

VII. Describe test administration, which includes:

    A. Location

    B. Date

    C. Resources
- People
- Equipment
- Supplies
- Software
- Test data
- Computer time
- Facilities

    D. Schedule

    E. Budget

    F. Responsibilities

    G. Training or skill requirements

    H. Documentation

    I. Test case libraries and standards

VIII. Describe requirements/specifications, which include:

    A. Inputs

    B. Outputs

    C. Processes and functions

    D. Interfaces

    E. Data structures and relationships

    F. Security

IX. Describe test design, which includes:

    A. Incremental testing, like:
- Top-down testing
- Bottom-up testing

    B. Non–incremental testing

X. Describe test strategy, which includes:
    A. Black box (data-driven) testing
    B. White box (logic-driven) testing

XI. Describe test techniques, which include:
    A. Logic test techniques
    B. Data test techniques

XII. Describe test cases, which include:
    A. Functionality
    B. Security
    C. Storage
    D. Documentation
    E. Backup and recovery
    F. Stress/threshold
    G. Volume
    H. Response time

XIII. Present evaluation criteria, which include:
    A. Test data
    B. Test conditions
    C. Expected results

XIV. Describe test execution, which includes:
    A. Test procedures regarding:
        • Input
        • Output
        • Control
    B. Tracking regarding:
        • Cases
        • Results
        • Recording

XV. Prepare glossary

XVI. Attach appendixes

TEST REPORT FORM OVERVIEW

I. DESCRIPTION

- Describes procedures and techniques including unit tests, test drivers, and inbound and outbound inputs (when boundaries exist)
- Compares "actuals" with "expected" outcomes, including discrepancies between performance requirements and actual performance
- Documents test results for test cases used

II. OBJECTIVES

- Ensure test plan compliance
- Identify problems and anomalies found during testing
- Support analysis of test results
- Recommend follow-on activities

III. ORGANIZATION

- Refer to Application Programmers (1.1.3.2), Testers (1.2.7), and Project Manager (1.6) in the Organization and Responsibilities Chart

IV. SCHEDULE

- Refer to the Code and Test (6.0), Verification/Validation (7.0), Integration (8.0), Conversion (9.0), and Installation and Implementation (10.0) phases of the Software Life Cycle Chart

TEST REPORT FORM

DATE: May 23, 19XX

END-ITEM IDENTIFICATION
OVRTBASE

END-ITEM DESCRIPTION
Overtime Baseline Pay

TEST #
5B-XX

TEST DATE
05/20/XX

TEST TIME
1132

STATUS
Failure

PROBLEM REPORT #
5B-XXXY

HARDWARE
HW-XXXX

SOFTWARE
SF-XXXY

TEST STEP #
7C-1XX

 # OF ATTEMPTS
3

ATTEMPT OUTCOME
Three times over
regular baseline
pay

WITNESS NAME
C. Coeule

ANOMALIES/CONSTRAINTS
Upper limit of three
times shown instead of two

IMPACT
Invalid amount,
so overtime
not added to
paycheck

RECOMMENDATIONS
Change in code to
match upper limit
of two times

TEST REPORT FORM

Date:

<u>END-ITEM IDENTIFICATION</u>   <u>END-ITEM DESCRIPTION</u>   <u>TEST #</u>

<u>TEST DATE</u>   <u>TEST TIME</u>   <u>STATUS</u>   <u>PROBLEM REPORT #</u>

<u>HARDWARE</u>   <u>SOFTWARE</u>   <u>TEST STEP #</u>   <u># OF ATTEMPTS</u>

<u>ATTEMPT OUTCOME</u>   <u>WITNESS NAME</u>   .<u>ANOMALIES/CONSTRAINTS</u>

<u>IMPACT</u>   <u>RECOMMENDATIONS</u>

HIERARCHY INPUT–PROCESS–OUTPUT (HIPO) DOCUMENTATION OVERVIEW

I. DESCRIPTION

- Illustrates the data and functions performed on that data and the corresponding output of those functions graphically and in a top-down manner

II. OBJECTIVES

- Simplify and clarify program design and logic
- Improve documentation methods

III. ORGANIZATION

- Refer to Application Programmers (1.1.3.2) and Project Manager (1.6) in the Organization and Responsibilities Chart

IV. SCHEDULE

- Refer to the Code and Test (6.0), Maintenance (11.0), and Enhancements (12.0) phases of the Software Life Cycle Chart

HIERARCHY CHART

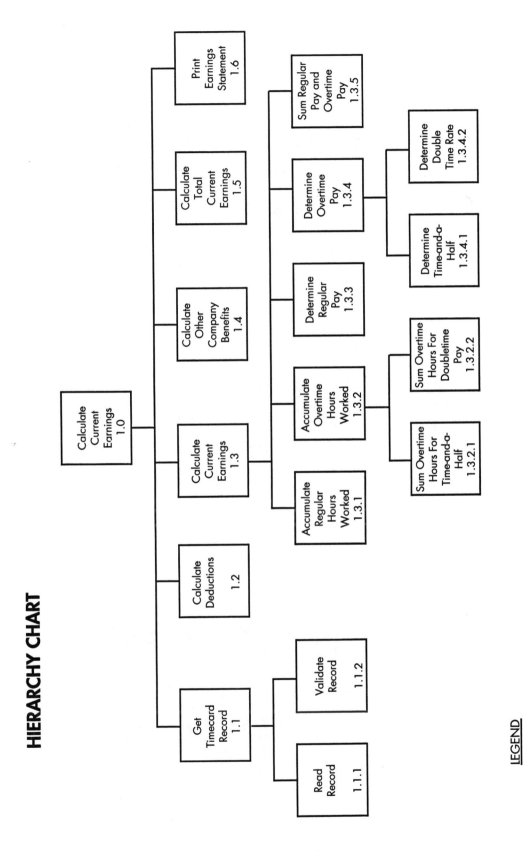

LEGEND

☐ MODULE

Calculate Current Earnings 1.0

Get Timecard Record 1.1

Calculate Deductions 1.2

Calculate Current Earnings 1.3

Calculate Other Company Benefits 1.4

Calculate Total Current Earnings 1.5

Print Earnings Statement 1.6

Read Record 1.1.1

Validate Record 1.1.2

Accumulate Regular Hours Worked 1.3.1

Accumulate Overtime Hours Worked 1.3.2

Determine Regular Pay 1.3.3

Determine Overtime Pay 1.3.4

Sum Regular Pay and Overtime Pay 1.3.5

Sum Overtime Hours For Time-and-a-Half 1.3.2.1

Sum Overtime Hours For Doubletime Pay 1.3.2.2

Determine Time-and-a-Half 1.3.4.1

Determine Double Time Rate 1.3.4.2

IPO CHART

MODULE: CALCULATE CURRENT EARNINGS (1.3)

INPUT	PROCESSING	OUTPUT
1. REGULAR HOURS PER DAY 2. OVERTIME HOURS PER DAY 3. HOURLY PAY RATE 4. TOTAL REGULAR HOURS 5. TIME-AND-A-HALF HOURLY RATE 6. DOUBLE-TIME HOURLY RATE 7. TOTAL REGULAR PAY 8. TOTAL OVERTIME PAY 9. TOTAL TIME-AND-A-HALF HOURS 10. TOTAL DOUBLE-TIME HOURS	1.3.1 ACCUMULATE REGULAR HOURS WORKED 1.3.2 ACCUMULATE OVERTIME HOURS WORKED 1.3.3 DETERMINE REGULAR PAY 1.3.4 DETERMINE OVERTIME PAY 1.3.5 SUM REGULAR PAY AND OVERTIME PAY	1. CURRENT EARNINGS FILE 2. PAYROLL MASTER

Chapter 7
Verification/Validation

VERIFICATION/VALIDATION PLAN OVERVIEW

I. DESCRIPTION

- Provides software verification/validation tools and techniques that increase confidence in software quality
- Verification ensures that
  - Design is consistent with requirements
  - Code is consistent with design
  - Testing is consistent with requirements
- Acceptance testing repeats functional testing under the auspices of quality assurance.
- Validation ensures that
  - Code is consistent with requirements
  - System performance is consistent with requirements

II. OBJECTIVES

- Demonstrate and document that all requirements have been met, including:
  - Functional specifications adherence
  - Qualification methodologies
- Provide software that is at a minimum:
  - Functional
  - Reliable
  - Efficient
  - Portable
  - Robust
  - Cost-effective
- Identify tool types, including:
  - Tracing aids
  - Data-flow analyzers

— Inspections
— Walkthroughs
— Test generators

III. ORGANIZATION

- Refer to Supervisor of Programming (1.1.3), Systems Programmers (1.1.3.1), Application Programmers (1.1.3.2), Manager of Technical Support (1.2), Configuration Management Specialists (1.2.4), Quality-Assurance Specialists (1.2.5), Testers (1.2.7), and Project Manager (1.6) in the Organization and Responsibilities Chart

IV. SCHEDULE

- Refer to the Requirements (2.0), Alternatives (3.0), Specifications (4.0), Design (5.0), Code and Test (6.0), and Validation/Verification (7.0) phases of the Software Life Cycle Chart

VERIFICATION/VALIDATION PLAN

I. Present title page, which includes:
   A. Document title
   B. Document number
   C. Original release date
   D. Current release date
   E. Current revision number
   F. Appropriate signatures and date

II. Present modifications sheet, which includes:
   A. Sequentially numbered list of changes
   B. Explanation of changes
   C. Page numbers of changes
   D. Appropriate signatures and date

III. Present table of contents, which includes:
   A. Section headings
   B. Chapter titles
   C. Chapter subtitles
   D. Relevant page numbers

IV. Present executive summary, which includes:
   A. Overview
   B. Principal features

V. Present introduction, which includes:
   A. Goals
   B. Scope
   C. Objectives, like:
      • Technical
      • Business
   D. Background information

VI. Define test environments, including:
   A. Software evaluation
   B. Software enhancements

    C. Regression testing

    D. Design-based test data

    E. Physical structure-based test data

    F. Independent testing

VII. Define test levels, including:

    A. Branch testing

    B. Path testing

    C. Reduction testing

VIII. Define inspection requirements, including:

    A. Formal, disciplined manual analysis

    B. Data declarations, such as:

        • Declared variables

        • Initialized variables

        • Correct attribute assignments

        • Comment explanations

IX. Conduct hardware test, including:

    A. Certification

    B. Uncertified negotiations

X. Define test scenarios, including:

    A. Internal structures

    B. Internal functions

    C. Static analysis, like:

        • Error detection through product examination

    D. Dynamic analysis, like:

        • Detection of classes of errors (e.g., erroneous sequencing)

XI. Define qualification processes, including:

    A. Acceptance testing

    B. Proof of correctness

    C. Performance testing

    D. Criticality levels

    E. Tolerance testing

    F. Functional correctness

XII. Prepare glossary

XIII. Attach appendixes

VERIFICATION/VALIDATION TEST COMPLETION REPORT FORM OVERVIEW

I. DESCRIPTION

- Provides baseline test completion report

II. OBJECTIVES

- Identify whether test procedures and corresponding configuration should change when modifications are made to final software before retesting
- Keep management aware of procedure development activities

III. ORGANIZATION

- Refer to Testers (1.2.7) in the Organization and Responsibilities Chart

IV. SCHEDULE

- Refer to the Verification/Validation (7.0), Integration (8.0), Conversion (9.0), and Installation and Implementation (10.0) phases of the Software Life Cycle Chart

VERIFICATION/VALIDATION TEST COMPLETION REPORT FORM

DATE: September 10, 19XX

SENIOR ENGINEER: E. E. Degrey

TEST IDENTIFICATION #: 3X-XXX

TEST DESIGN FILE DIRECTORY: TDFX-XXXX

TEST PROCEDURE FILE DIRECTORY: TPFY-YYYY

DEVELOPMENT EFFORT   MODIFIED TEST-BED SIMULATION
Yes   No

MODIFIED SOFTWARE   COMPATIBLE WITH OPERATING SYSTEM SOFTWARE
No   Yes

MEMORY MAP CHANGE DESCRIPTION   DEVELOPMENT EFFORT VERSION #
None   8X-XXXY

MODIFIED TEST-BED SIMULATION VERSION #   PROBLEM REPORT #
None   7B-XXXZ

SPECIAL TOOLS DESCRIPTION   REMARKS
None

VERIFICATION/VALIDATION TEST COMPLETION REPORT FORM

DATE:

SENIOR ENGINEER:

TEST IDENTIFICATION #:

TEST DESIGN FILE DIRECTORY:

TEST PROCEDURE FILE DIRECTORY:

DEVELOPMENT EFFORT   MODIFIED TEST-BED SIMULATION

MODIFIED SOFTWARE   COMPATIBLE WITH OPERATING SYSTEM SOFTWARE

MEMORY MAP CHANGE DESCRIPTION   DEVELOPMENT EFFORT VERSION #

MODIFIED TEST BED SIMULATION VERSION #   PROBLEM REPORT #

SPECIAL TOOLS DESCRIPTION   REMARKS

VERIFICATION/VALIDATION TEST CHECKLIST OVERVIEW

I. DESCRIPTION

- Provides list of test and performance activities

II. OBJECTIVE

- Ensure that software specification testing is complete and configuration control is in place

III. ORGANIZATION

- Refer to Systems Analysts (1.1.1.2), Systems Programmers (1.1.3.1), Application Programmers (1.1.3.2), Quality-Assurance Specialists (1.2.5), and Testers (1.2.7) in the Organization and Responsibilities Chart

IV. SCHEDULE

- Refer to the Verification/Validation phase (7.0) of the Software Life Cycle Chart

VERIFICATION/VALIDATION TEST CHECKLIST

I. Identify and document verification/validation requirements, including:
- ☐ Test of software specifications
- ☐ Adherence to standards and conventions
- ☐ Requirements satisfaction
- ☐ No extraneous functions

II. Identify and document verification/validation testing, including:
- ☐ Procedures have been defined and followed
- ☐ Adherence to design
- ☐ Software compliance with Functional Specifications document
- ☐ Complete regression testing
- ☐ Complete integrity testing
- ☐ Complete evolution checking
- ☐ Complete appropriateness checking

III. Identify and document verification/validation configuration control, including:
- ☐ Software
- ☐ Hardware
- ☐ Drawings

IV. Identify and document verification/validation administrative control, including:
- ☐ Completion reviews held
- ☐ Completion reports filled and accepted
- ☐ Tool acquisition completion
- ☐ Identification of long lead-time activities

Chapter 8

Integration

SUBSYSTEM TEST REPORT FORM OVERVIEW

I. DESCRIPTION

- Documents test results
- Describes tests and techniques used
- Compares ''actuals'' with ''expected'' outcomes

II. OBJECTIVE

- Test a group of software programs constituting a single functional area to demonstrate that integrity is maintained for data relationships and program interfaces

III. ORGANIZATION

- Refer to Quality-Assurance Specialists (1.2.5), Testers (1.2.7), and Project Manager (1.6) in the Organization and Responsibilities Chart

IV. SCHEDULE

- Refer to the Integration (8.0), Conversion (9.0), and Installation and Implementation (10.0) phases of the Software Life Cycle Chart

SUBSYSTEM TEST REPORT FORM

SUBSYSTEM IDENTIFICATION
Vactn

SOFTWARE PROGRAM IDENTIFICATION
Vacatot

CONDITION #	DESCRIPTION	PROCEDURE	EXPECTATIONS
5XX-1	Generate paycheck hardcopy time available/ expended	Run simulation	Simulation error for invalid employee id

ACTUALS	TESTED BY	DATE	REMARKS
Error discovered	J. Farley	07/10/XX	

SUBSYSTEM TEST REPORT FORM

SUBSYSTEM IDENTIFICATION   SOFTWARE PROGRAM IDENTIFICATION

CONDITION #   DESCRIPTION   PROCEDURE   EXPECTATIONS

ACTUALS   TESTED BY   DATE   REMARKS

SYSTEM TEST REPORT FORM OVERVIEW

I. DESCRIPTION

- Documents test results
- Describes tests and techniques used
- Compares "actuals" with "expected" outcomes

II. OBJECTIVE

- Test the entire system to demonstrate identification and interaction, including:
  — Subsystems
  — Interfaces
  — Data files
  — Database files
  — Directives
  — Procedures
  — Documentation

III. ORGANIZATION

- Refer to Quality-Assurance Specialists (1.2.5), Testers (1.2.7), and Project Manager (1.6) in the Organization and Responsibilities Chart

IV. SCHEDULE

- Refer to the Integration (8.0), Conversion (9.0), and Installation and Implementation (10.0) phases of the Software Life Cycle Chart

SYSTEM TEST REPORT FORM

CONDITION #
7-XX-5

DESCRIPTION
Generate database
update of employee
social security
withholding according
to current structure

SUBSYSTEM IDENTIFICATION
Sswith

PROCEDURE
Verify thru database
report and online
capability

EXPECTATIONS
Database updated

ACTUALS
Update generated on
screen, but not on
hardcopy

TESTED BY
A. Dickinson

DATE
10-05-XX

REMARKS
Check report generator

SYSTEM TEST REPORT FORM

CONDITION #   DESCRIPTION   SUBSYSTEM IDENTIFICATION

PROCEDURE   EXPECTATIONS   ACTUALS

TESTED BY   DATE   REMARKS

Chapter 9

Conversion

SYSTEM CONVERSION PLAN OVERVIEW

I. DESCRIPTION

- Establishes requirements, procedures, and special programming, including:
  — New master records

  — New file-build programs

  — New forms generation

  — New storage devices and facilities

  — Data purification effort review

II. OBJECTIVES

- Prepare for system implementation, including:
  — Conceptual approach

  — Strategies

  — Tactics
- Document details for converting to a new system, including:
  — Conversion activities control

  — Rationale for additional programs

III. ORGANIZATION

- Refer to Manager of Development (1.1), Supervisor of Programming (1.1.3, 1.4.2), Systems Programmers (1.1.3.1, 1.4.2.1), Application Programmers (1.1.3.2, 1.4.2.2), Manager of Technical Support (1.2), Configuration Management Specialists (1.2.4), Quality-Assurance Specialists (1.2.5), Testers (1.2.7), Manager of Sustaining (1.4), Supervisor of Analysis (1.4.1), Systems Analysts (1.4.1.2), Methods Analysts (1.4.1.3), and Project Manager (1.6) in the Organization and Responsibilities Chart

IV. SCHEDULE

- Refer to the Specifications (4.0), Design (5.0), Code and Test (6.0), Verification/Validation (7.0), Integration (8.0), and Conversion (9.0) phases of the Software Life Cycle Chart

SYSTEM CONVERSION PLAN

I. Present title page, which includes:
   A. Document title
   B. Document number
   C. Original release date
   D. Current release date
   E. Current revision number
   F. Appropriate signatures and date

II. Present modifications sheet, which includes:
   A. Sequentially numbered list of changes
   B. Explanation of changes
   C. Page numbers of changes
   D. Appropriate signatures and date

III. Present table of contents, which includes:
   A. Section headings
   B. Chapter titles
   C. Chapter subtitles
   D. Relevant page numbers

IV. Present executive summary, which includes:
   A. Overview
   B. Principal features

V. Present introduction, which includes:
   A. Goals
   B. Scope
   C. Objectives, like
      • Technical
      • Business
   D. Background information

VI. Provide program identification and documentation, which include:
   A. Changes and edits required

B. No changes or edits required
C. Policies and procedures
D. Standards and conventions
E. Access security
F. Vendor selection

VII. Provide operational requirements, which include:
A. Costs
B. Schedules
C. Personnel
D. Equipment
E. Software
F. Supplies
G. Facilities

VIII. Prepare glossary

IX. Attach appendixes

SYSTEM CONVERSION CHECKLIST OVERVIEW

I. DESCRIPTION

- Provides conversion preparation and activities list

II. OBJECTIVES

- Identify resource requirements
- Document plans
- Address processes or changes or both

III. ORGANIZATION

- Refer to Supervisor of Programming (1.1.3), Systems Programmers (1.1.3.1, 1.4.2.1), Application Programmers (1.1.3.2, 1.4.2.2), Supervisor of Analysis (1.4.1), and Systems Analysts (1.4.1.2) in the Organization and Responsibilities Chart

IV. SCHEDULE

- Refer to the Specifications (4.0), Design (5.0), Code and Test (6.0), Verification/Validation (7.0), Integration (8.0), and Conversion (9.0) phases of the Software Life Cycle Chart

SYSTEM CONVERSION CHECKLIST

I. Define and document requirements for system conversion, including:
- ☐ Statement of Work, such as:
  - ☐ Signature and date approved
- ☐ Resources, such as:
  - ☐ Time
  - ☐ Equipment
  - ☐ Labor
  - ☐ Cost
- ☐ Conversion criteria
- ☐ Standards
- ☐ Organizational plan, such as:
  - ☐ Signature and date approved
- ☐ Training plan
- ☐ Facilities layout, such as:
  - ☐ Signature and date approved

II. Address changes for system conversion, including:
- ☐ Process(es)
- ☐ Procedure
- ☐ Operating system
- ☐ Software
- ☐ Hardware
- ☐ Programming language
- ☐ Network architecture
- ☐ File media
- ☐ Vendor

III. Identify and document miscellaneous areas, including:
- ☐ Upper-management and user-community support
- ☐ Target environment
- ☐ Current process(es) impacts during the conversion
- ☐ Delivery schedule dates
- ☐ Complexity factors
- ☐ Risks and associated impacts

DATA CONVERSION PLAN OVERVIEW

I. DESCRIPTION

- Achieves a flexible environment for data conversion, including:
  — Policies, procedures, processes, methodologies, and standards
  — Simplification and improvement areas
  — Impact areas
  — Reduced data repositories

II. OBJECTIVE

- Ensure data conversion management and standardization

III. ORGANIZATION

- Refer to Manager of Technical Support (1.2), Database Administrators (1.2.3), Configuration Management Specialists (1.2.4), Manager of Sustaining (1.4), Supervisor of Analysis (1.4.1), Database Analysts (1.4.1.1), Systems Analysts (1.4.1.2), and Project Manager (1.6) in the Organization and Responsibilities Chart

IV. SCHEDULE

- Refer to the Specifications (4.0), Design (5.0), Code and Test (6.0), Verification/Validation (7.0), Integration (8.0), and Conversion (9.0) phases of the Software Life Cycle Chart

DATA CONVERSION PLAN

I. Present title page, which includes:
- A. Document title
- B. Document number
- C. Original release date
- D. Current release date
- E. Current revision number
- F. Appropriate signatures and date

II. Present modifications sheet, which includes:
- A. Sequentially numbered list of changes
- B. Explanation of changes
- C. Page numbers of changes
- D. Appropriate signatures and date

III. Present table of contents, which includes:
- A. Section headings
- B. Chapter titles
- C. Chapter subtitles
- D. Relevant page numbers

IV. Present executive summary, which includes:
- A. Overview
- B. Principal features

V. Present introduction, which includes
- A. Goals
- B. Scope
- C. Objectives, like
  - Technical
  - Business
- D. Background information

VI. Provide track and log discrepancy reports, including:
   A. Problem reports
   B. Interface revisions

VII. Establish security and documentation, including:
   - Test data generation
   - Test output and data files
   - Compare "actuals" with "expected" outcomes

VIII. Coordinate data/database interfaces, including:
   A. Data definitions
   B. Data dictionary
   C. Database control
   D. Database maintenance

IX. Coordinate library functions, including:
   A. Code changes
   B. Backup copies
   C. System generations
   D. Record keeping

X. Prepare glossary

XI. Attach appendixes

DATA CONVERSION CHECKLIST OVERVIEW

I. DESCRIPTION

- Provides list of requirements, definitions, standards, and performance for data conversion activity

II. OBJECTIVES

- Ensure that
  - Functionalities have been identified
  - Relationships have been defined
  - Environment is cohesive

III. ORGANIZATION

- Refer to Systems Librarians (1.2.1), Database Administrators (1.2.3), Supervisor of Analysis (1.4.1), Database Analysts (1.4.1.1), and Systems Analysts (1.4.1.2) in the Organization and Responsibilities Chart

IV. SCHEDULE

- Refer to the Specifications (4.0), Design (5.0), Code and Test (6.0), Verification/Validation (7.0), Integration (8.0), and Conversion (9.0) phases of the Software Life Cycle Chart

DATA CONVERSION CHECKLIST

I. Establish, identify, and maintain data conversion requirements, including:
- ☐ Cohesive database environment
- ☐ Business rules and processes
- ☐ System interfaces
- ☐ Redundancy reduction and elimination
- ☐ Access security levels

II. Create and maintain data conversion definitions and standards, including:
- ☐ Naming conventions/standards for processes
- ☐ Naming conventions/standards for data elements
- ☐ Toolset definitions
- ☐ Data dictionary elements
- ☐ Data relationships
- ☐ Database relationships

III. Address data conversion performance, including:
- ☐ Database performance reporting
- ☐ Database audit trails

Chapter 10

Installation and Implementation

INSTALLATION AND IMPLEMENTATION PLAN OVERVIEW

I. DESCRIPTION

- Identifies provisions necessary to meet with functional requirements and design as defined in specifications and convert those programs, including:
  - Computer software
  - Configuration
  - Successful testing
  - Data center facilities
  - Training
  - Traceability
  - Contingency plans
- The last opportunity to modify and fine-tune the plan to ensure a smooth transfer and transition to the converted application

II. OBJECTIVES

- Provide adequate preparation for installation and implementation, including:
  - Organizational roles and responsibilities
  - Upper-management commitment
  - Freezing and block-pointing programs to be converted
  - Testing those programs
  - Training
  - Preparing for implementation

III. ORGANIZATION

- Refer to Supervisor of Analysis (1.1.1, 1.4.1), Configuration Management Specialists (1.2.4), Manager of Sustaining (1.4), Systems Analysts (1.4.1.2), Methods Analysts (1.4.1.3), Supervisor of Programming (1.4.2), Systems Programmers (1.4.2.1), Application Programmers (1.4.2.2), and Project Manager (1.6) in the Organization and Responsibilities Chart

IV. SCHEDULE

- Refer to the Design (5.0), Code and Test (6.0), Verification/Validation (7.0), Integration (8.0), Conversion (9.0), and Installation and Implementation (10.0) phases of the Software Life Cycle Chart

INSTALLATION AND IMPLEMENTATION PLAN

I. Present title page, which includes:
  - A. Document title
  - B. Document number
  - C. Original release date
  - D. Current release date
  - E. Current revision number
  - F. Appropriate signatures and date

II. Present modifications sheet, which includes:
  - A. Sequentially numbered list of all changes
  - B. Explanation of changes
  - C. Page numbers of changes
  - D. Appropriate signatures and date

III. Present table of contents, which includes:
  - A. Section headings
  - B. Chapter titles
  - C. Chapter subtitles
  - D. Relevant page numbers

IV. Present executive summary, which includes:
  - A. Overview
  - B. Principal features

V. Present introduction, which includes:
  - A. Goals
  - B. Scope
  - C. Objectives, like
    - Technical
    - Business
  - D. Background information

VI. Identify and resolve installation and implementation plan issues, including:
- A. System-generated errors
- B. Processing bottlenecks
- C. Testing and freeze packages
- D. Hardware performance
- E. Software performance
- F. Complete training of personnel
- G. Revised plan where necessary

VII. Identify operational requirements, including:
- A. Costs
- B. Schedules
- C. Personnel
- D. Equipment
- E. Software
- F. Supplies
- G. Facilities

VIII. Prepare glossary

IX. Attach appendixes

INSTALLATION AND IMPLEMENTATION PACKAGE FORM OVERVIEW

I. DESCRIPTION

- Provides information required for each work package to control software package delivery

II. OBJECTIVE

- Keep software program records current and up to date

III. ORGANIZATION

- Refer to Systems Programmers (1.1.3.1, 1.4.2.1), Application Programmers (1.1.3.2, 1.4.2.2), Systems Librarians (1.2.1), Testers (1.2.7), Job Schedulers (1.3.2.1), and Project Manager (1.6) in the Organization and Responsibilities Chart

IV. SCHEDULE

- Refer to the Installation and Implementation (10.0), Maintenance (11.0), and Enhancements (12.0) phases of the Software Life Cycle Chart

INSTALLATION AND IMPLEMENTATION PACKAGE FORM

PACKAGE TITLE: BENEFITS
REVISION #: A
DESCRIPTION OF APPLICATION: BENEFITS AS REFLECTED BY CURRENT YEAR
LABOR CONTRACT
DATE: JUNE 16, 19XX
PREPARED BY: L. JONES
ORGANIZATION: Testers

SOFTWARE PROGRAM IDENTIFICATION	REVISION #	DESCRIPTION
Medbenef	A	Medical benefits

SOURCE LIST	TEST #	TEST-RUN DOCUMENT #	FLOWCHART #
MB1XX	2	2XXX-X	2XX-X

PERFORMED BY	PLANNED COMPLETION DATE	APPROVED BY
J. Jackson	06-15-XX	O. Pearson

DATE APPROVED
06-15-XX

INSTALLATION AND IMPLEMENTATION PACKAGE FORM

PACKAGE TITLE:
REVISION #:
DESCRIPTION OF APPLICATION:
DATE:
PREPARED BY:
ORGANIZATION:

SOFTWARE PROGRAM IDENTIFICATION   REVISION #   DESCRIPTION

SOURCE LIST   TEST #   TEST-RUN DOCUMENT #   FLOWCHART #

PERFORMED BY   PLANNED COMPLETION DATE   APPROVED BY

DATE APPROVED

INSTALLATION AND IMPLEMENTATION CHECKLIST OVERVIEW

I. DESCRIPTION

- Addresses operational and administrative installation and implementation

II. OBJECTIVES

- Identify operational requirements and interfaces
- Assign roles and responsibilities for hardware and software assignments
- Evaluate system performance

III. ORGANIZATION

- Refer to Systems Programmers (1.1.3.1, 1.4.2.1), Application Programmers (1.1.3.2, 1.4.2.2), Testers (1.2.7), Supervisor of Analysis (1.4.1), and Systems Analysts (1.4.1.2) in the Organization and Responsibilities Chart

IV. SCHEDULE

- Refer to Design (5.0), Code and Test (6.0), Verification/Validation (7.0), Integration (8.0), Conversion (9.0), and Installation and Implementation (10.0) phases of the Software Life Cycle Chart

INSTALLATION AND IMPLEMENTATION CHECKLIST

    I. Address staffing requirements, including:

- ☐ Hardware training
- ☐ Software training
- ☐ Backup personnel
- ☐ Roles and responsibilities
- ☐ User involvement

   II. Address security issues, including:

- ☐ Control of proprietary information
- ☐ Accessibility to proprietary work areas

  III. Address equipment issues, including:

- ☐ Hardware
    - ☐ On site
    - ☐ Tested
    - ☐ Validated
- ☐ Changes to hardware
- ☐ Equipment capacity to handle peak workloads
- ☐ Sufficient machine time for conversion efforts

  IV. Address software issues, including:

- ☐ Installation completeness and performance expectations
- ☐ Test and validation of interfaces
- ☐ Identification and documentation of changes
- ☐ Backup and recovery procedure
- ☐ Performance expectations

   V. Address converted application issues, including:

- ☐ Allocation of adequate testing time
- ☐ Consistency between software and hardware documentation
- ☐ Identification and documentation of changes
- ☐ Validation of system performance
- ☐ Perform demonstration with dummy data

  VI. Address data/database issues, including:

- ☐ Clean up and testing of converted files
- ☐ Ensure test-plan maintenance integrity of converted files after processing live production data
- ☐ Identification and documentation of changes

VII. Address administrative issues, including:
   - ☐ Hold management reviews with the appropriate organizations
   - ☐ Problem reporting mechanisms exist
   - ☐ Identification and documentation of changes
   - ☐ Evaluation of how system reacts when unanticipated events arise

VIII. Address facilities issues, including:
   - ☐ Operable and in place, like:
     - ☐ Power
     - ☐ Supplies
     - ☐ Heating
     - ☐ Ventilation
     - ☐ Air conditioning
   - ☐ Schedule approval for multiple and/or pilot sites
   - ☐ Facilities acceptability

SUSTAINING

Chapter 11

Maintenance

PROGRAMMING CHECKLIST OVERVIEW

I. DESCRIPTION

- Provides procedures, controls, and documentation list for programming maintenance

II. OBJECTIVE

- Provide accurate transaction handling for editing, data changes, and software maintenance

III. ORGANIZATION

- Refer to Supervisor of Programming (1.1.3, 1.4.2), Systems Programmers (1.1.3.1, 1.4.2.1), and Application Programmers (1.1.3.2, 1.4.2.2) in the Organization and Responsibilities Chart

IV. SCHEDULE

- Refer to the Installation and Implementation (10.0), and Maintenance (11.0) phases of the Software Life Cycle Chart

PROGRAMMING CHECKLIST

   I. Establish procedures for programming maintenance, including:
- ☐ Planned and unplanned change verifications
- ☐ Maintenance transactions
- ☐ Diagnostics

  II. Establish controls for programming maintenance, including:
- ☐ Maintenance transactions
- ☐ Standards and their adherence
- ☐ Authorization levels access

 III. Provide complete, accurate, and current documentation for programming maintenance, including:
- ☐ Text
- ☐ Drawings
- ☐ Flowcharts
- ☐ Diagrams

 IV. Review other programming maintenance areas, including:
- ☐ Open communication lines with the user
- ☐ Assigned maintenance roles and responsibilities
- ☐ Rejection corrections in work
- ☐ Meaning of error messages
- ☐ Special features and conditions

FACILITY USAGE CHECKLIST OVERVIEW

I. DESCRIPTION

- Provides facilities usage requirements list

II. OBJECTIVE

- Identify facility usage requirements, including:
  — Layout
  — Equipment
  — Utilities
  — Budget

III. ORGANIZATION

- Refer to Supervisor of Computer Operations (1.3.1) in the Organization and Responsibilities Chart

IV. SCHEDULE

- Refer to the Installation and Implementation (10.0) and Maintenance (11.0) phases of the Software Life Cycle Chart

FACILITY USAGE CHECKLIST

I. Provide accountability for facility usage, including:
- ☐ Existing facilities usage
- ☐ Flexible facility usage (for more than one purpose)
- ☐ New site location, to include:
  - ☐ New construction
  - ☐ Renting
  - ☐ Leasing

II. Identify operational aspects for facility usage, including:
- ☐ Existing manpower usage
- ☐ Sufficient budget allocation
- ☐ Equipment set up
- ☐ Utilities turned on
- ☐ Identification of security restrictions

III. Comply with governing procedures and regulations, including:
- ☐ Safety
- ☐ Health
- ☐ Fire
- ☐ Electrical
- ☐ Mechanical
- ☐ Utilities
- ☐ Sanction of special codes or regulations

EQUIPMENT MAINTENANCE REPORT FORM OVERVIEW

I. DESCRIPTION

- Identifies equipment installation, replacement, and repair activities

II. OBJECTIVES

- Provide documentation and maintenance audit trail for performance monitoring

III. ORGANIZATION

- Refer to Supervisor of Computer Operations (1.3.1) in the Organization and Responsibilities Chart

IV. SCHEDULE

- Refer to the Maintenance (11.0) and Enhancements (12.0) phases of the Software Life Cycle Chart

EQUIPMENT MAINTENANCE REPORT FORM

DATE: June 23, 19XX

<u>HARDWARE</u>   <u>INSTALL</u>   <u>REPLACE</u>   <u>REPAIR</u>
Yes   Yes

<u>ID #</u>   <u>VERSION #</u>   <u>DESCRIPTION</u>   <u>ACRONYM/ABBREVIATION</u>
PC-XXXX   5XX   Personal   PC-486-XX
        computer

<u>MANUFACTURER IDENTIFICATION</u>   <u>LOCATION</u>   <u>INSTALLER</u>
6XX-XXXX-XX   Bldg 5-X   K. Duit

<u>BENEFITING ORGANIZATION</u>   <u>DATE</u>   <u>REMARKS</u>
Operations   05-17-XX

EQUIPMENT MAINTENANCE REPORT FORM

DATE:

<u>HARDWARE</u>   <u>INSTALL</u>   <u>REPLACE</u>   <u>REPAIR</u>

<u>ID #</u>   <u>VERSION #</u>   <u>DESCRIPTION</u>   <u>ACRONYM/ABBREVIATION</u>

<u>MANUFACTURER IDENTIFICATION</u>   <u>LOCATION</u>   <u>INSTALLER</u>

<u>BENEFITING ORGANIZATION</u>   <u>DATE</u>   <u>REMARKS</u>

Chapter 12

Enhancements

SYSTEM UPGRADE CHECKLIST OVERVIEW

I. DESCRIPTION

- Identifies whether upgrades are realistic, value-added, and cost effective

II. OBJECTIVES

- Provide better understanding of the system upgrade evaluation process, including:
  — Hardware
  — Software
  — Standards criteria

III. ORGANIZATION

- Refer to Configuration Management Specialists (1.2.4), Manager of Operations (1.3), Supervisor of Computer Operations (1.3.1), Manager of Sustaining (1.4), Supervisor of Analysis (1.4.1), and Systems Analysts (1.4.1.2) in the Organization and Responsibilities Chart

IV. SCHEDULE

- Refer to the Maintenance (11.0) and Enhancements (12.0) phases of the Software Life Cycle Chart

SYSTEM UPGRADE CHECKLIST

I. List and evaluate upgrade items, including:
- ☐ Hardware, such as:
    - ☐ Necessary upgrade
    - ☐ Desirable upgrade
- ☐ Software, such as:
    - ☐ Necessary upgrade
    - ☐ Desirable upgrade
- ☐ Peripherals, such as:
    - ☐ Necessary upgrade
    - ☐ Desirable upgrade

II. List upgrade items that are currently available, including:
- ☐ Hardware
- ☐ Software
- ☐ Peripherals

III. List and evaluate upgrade supplies, including:
- ☐ Consumable supplies (e.g., tape, punchcards)
- ☐ Nonconsumable supplies (e.g., tape cabinets, fireproof storage units)

IV. Identify and evaluate administrative areas, including:
- ☐ Service contracts
- ☐ Outsourcing resources
- ☐ Standards criteria
- ☐ Pricing review
- ☐ Purchased services meeting acceptance criteria
- ☐ Ease of installation
- ☐ Special considerations requiring installation
- ☐ Special terms and conditions list

SYSTEM PERFORMANCE GRAPHS OVERVIEW

I. DESCRIPTION

- Identifies visually how well the system is performing with respect to current benchmarks, including:
  — Budget
  — Labor hours
  — Equipment units

II. OBJECTIVES

- Establish system performance baseline
- Adjust system as required
- Aid in identifying risks and trends

III. ORGANIZATION

- Refer to Program Planners (1.2.6), Manager of Operations (1.3), Supervisor of Computer Operations (1.3.1), and Manager of Sustaining (1.4) in the Organization and Responsibilities Chart

IV. SCHEDULE

- Refer to the Installation and Implementation (10.0), Maintenance (11.0), and Enhancements (12.0) phases of the Software Life Cycle Chart

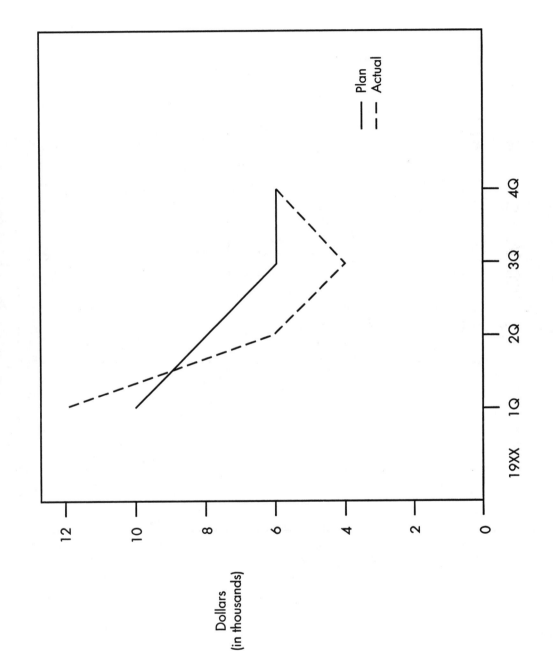

BUDGET PERFORMANCE GRAPH

Dollars
(in thousands)

12

10

8

6

4

2

0

19XX   1Q   2Q   3Q   4Q

Plan
Actual

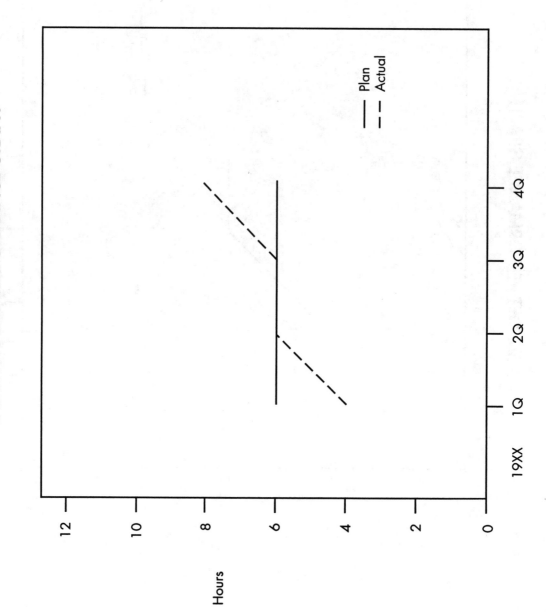

LABOR HOURS PERFORMANCE GRAPH

Hours

12
10
8
6
4
2
0

19XX   1Q   2Q   3Q   4Q

——— Plan
– – – Actual

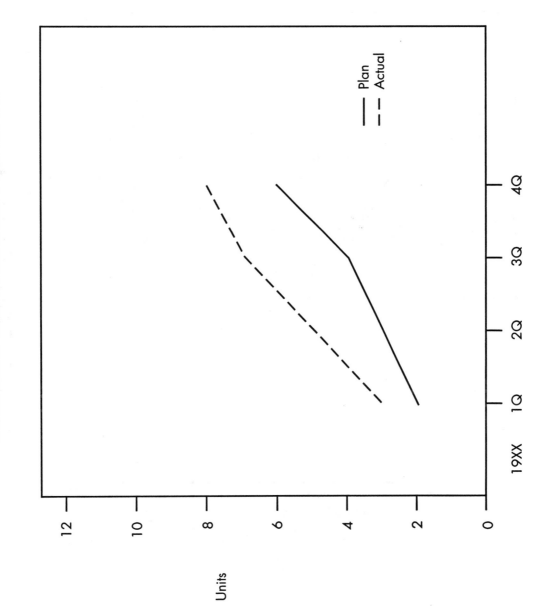

EQUIPMENT UNITS PERFORMANCE GRAPH

Units

12

10

8

6

4

2

0

19XX   1Q   2Q   3Q   4Q

——— Plan
— — Actual

CUMULATIVE BUDGET PERFORMANCE GRAPH

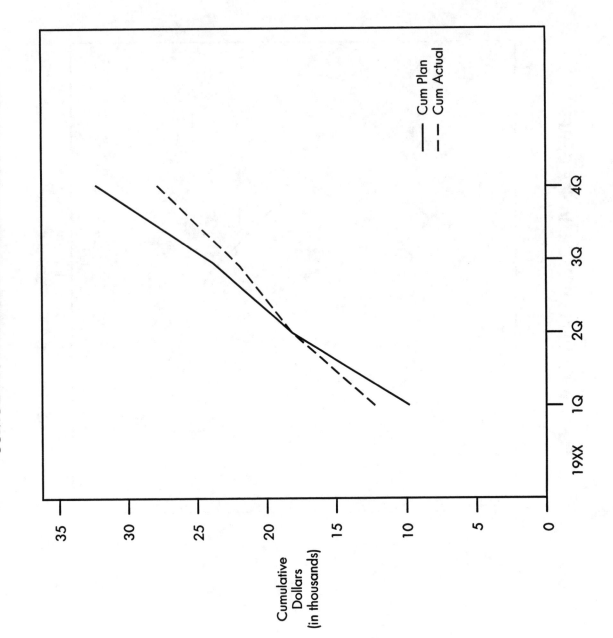

Cumulative
Dollars
(in thousands)

—— Cum Plan
— — Cum Actual

19XX   1Q   2Q   3Q   4Q

CUMULATIVE LABOR HOURS PERFORMANCE GRAPH

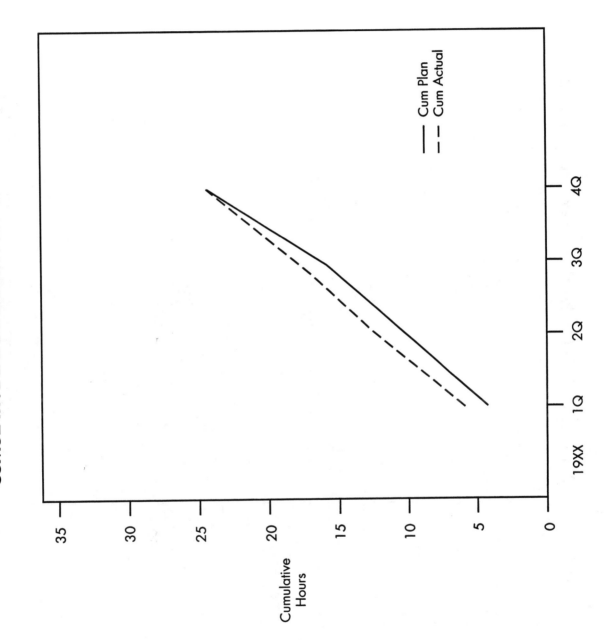

Cumulative
Hours

—— Cum Plan
— — Cum Actual

19XX   1Q   2Q   3Q   4Q

CUMULATIVE EQUIPMENT UNITS PERFORMANCE GRAPH

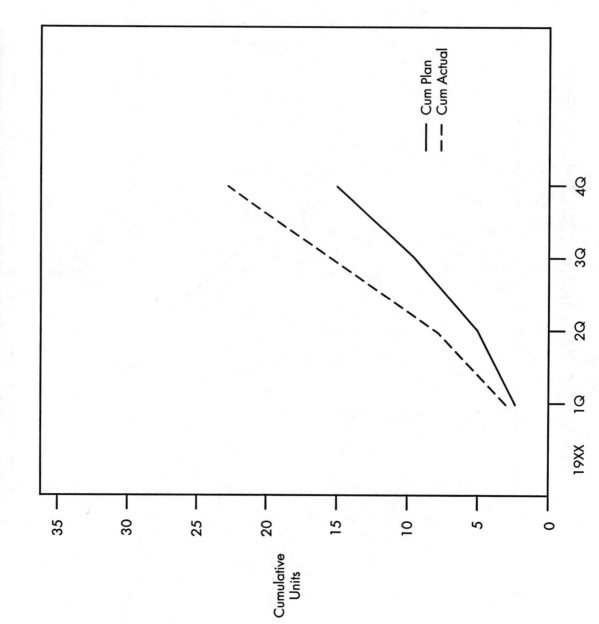

SYSTEM PRODUCTIVITY GRAPHS OVERVIEW

I. DESCRIPTION

- Identifies visually how well the system is performing with respect to current benchmarks, including:
  — Equipment state
  — Tuning
  — Software

II. OBJECTIVES

- Establish system performance baseline
- Adjust system as required
- Aid in identifying risks and trends

III. ORGANIZATION

- Refer to Program Planners (1.2.6), Manager of Operations (1.3), Supervisor of Computer Operations (1.3.1), and Manager of Sustaining (1.4) in the Organization and Responsibilities Chart

IV. SCHEDULE

- Refer to the Installation and Implementation (10.0), Maintenance (11.0), and Enhancements (12.0) phases of the Software Life Cycle Chart

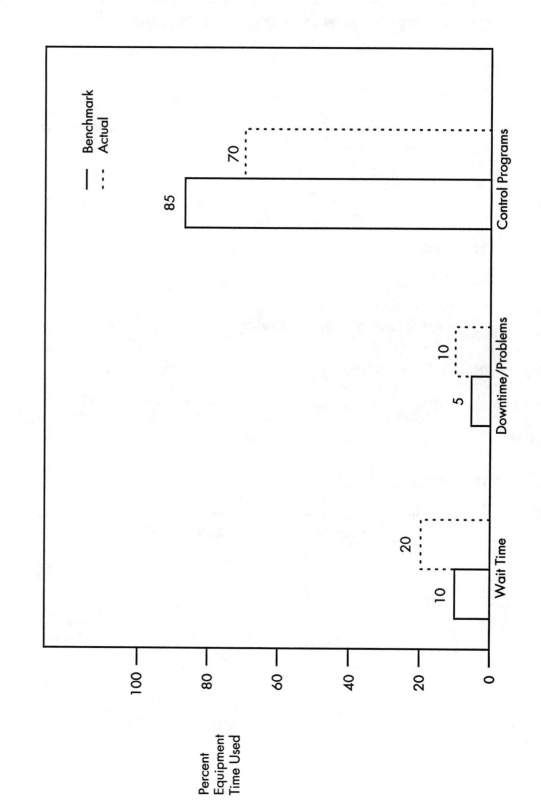

EQUIPMENT STATE PRODUCTIVITY

19XX First Quarter

Benchmark
Actual

Percent
Equipment
Time Used

Wait Time   Downtime/Problems   Control Programs

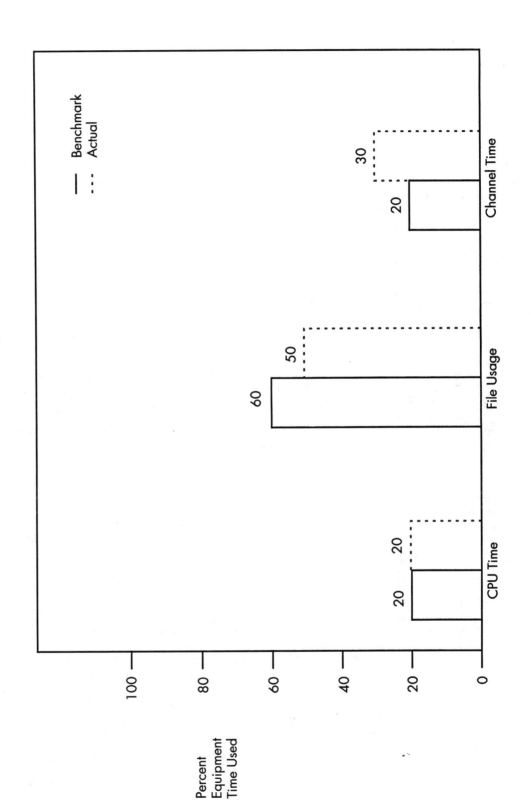

TUNING PRODUCTIVITY GRAPH

19XX First Quarter

Benchmark ———
Actual - - -

Percent
Equipment
Time Used

100
80
60
40
20
0

CPU Time
20
20

File Usage
60
50

Channel Time
30
20

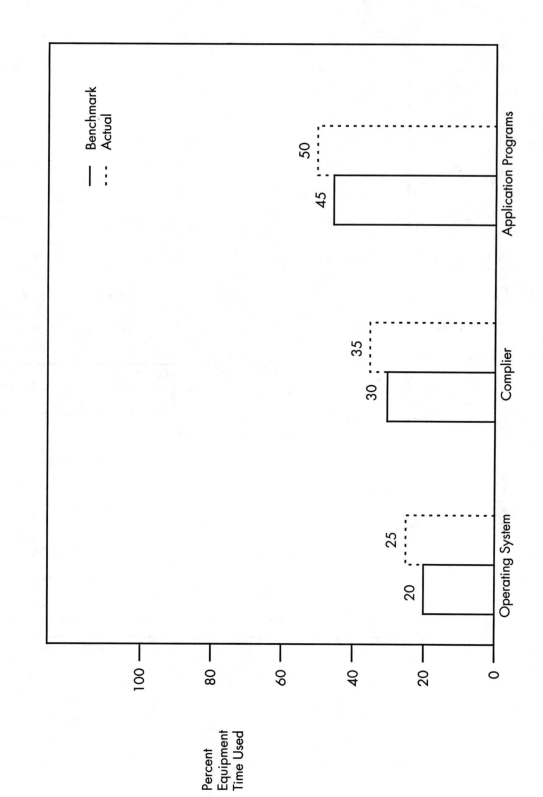

SOFTWARE PRODUCTIVITY GRAPH

19XX First Quarter

Benchmark
Actual

Percent
Equipment
Time Used

100

80

60

40

20

0

Operating System

20

25

Complier

30

35

Application Programs

45

50

SECTION III

OPERATIONS

Chapter 13

Data Center—
Operations

DATA CENTER—OPERATIONS PLAN OVERVIEW

I. DESCRIPTION

- Provides test bed for the validation of computing concepts in a real-life environment without having a complete system

II. OBJECTIVE

- Test the system "as delivered" and at operational levels, including:
  - Hardware
  - Software
  - Integration of hardware and software
  - Special equipment
  - Security
  - Network communications
  - Facilities

III. ORGANIZATION

- Refer to Supervisor of Programming (1.1.3), Manager of Technical Support (1.2), Configuration Management Specialists (1.2.4), Quality-Assurance Specialists (1.2.5), Testers (1.2.7), Manager of Operations (1.3), Supervisor of Computer Operations (1.3.1), Manager of Sustaining (1.4), and Project Manager (1.6) in the Organization and Responsibilities Chart

IV. SCHEDULE

- Refer to the Specifications (4.0), Design (5.0), Code and Test (6.0), Verification/Validation (7.0), Integration (8.0), Conversion (9.0), and Installation and Implementation (10.0) phases of the Software Life Cycle Chart

DATA CENTER—OPERATIONS PLAN

I. Present title page, which includes:
    A. Document title
    B. Document number
    C. Original release date
    D. Current release date
    E. Current revision number
    F. Appropriate signatures and date

II. Present modifications sheet, which includes:
    A. Sequentially numbered list of changes
    B. Explanation of changes
    C. Page numbers of changes
    D. Appropriate signatures and date

III. Present table of contents, which includes:
    A. Section headings
    B. Chapter titles
    C. Chapter subtitles
    D. Relevant page numbers

IV. Present executive summary, which includes:
    A. Overview
    B. Principal features

V. Present introduction, which includes:
    A. Goals
    B. Scope
    C. Objectives, like:
        • Technical
        • Business
    D. Background information

VI. Establish test site for environmental simulation, including:
    A. Congruency of realistic attributes reflecting system's operations

B. Determine test bed's ability to focus on software tested

C. Process software through test bed, including:
- Inputs
- Replications
- Diagnostics

D. Monitor software component testing, including:
- Intermediate outputs
- Replications
- Verification
- Diagnostics

E. Analyze test bed results
- Compare "actuals" with "expected" outcomes

VII. Present operational requirements, including:
A. Costs
B. Schedules
C. Personnel
D. Equipment
E. Software
F. Supplies
G. Facilities

VIII. Prepare glossary

IX. Attach appendixes

SYSTEM UTILIZATION LOG FORM OVERVIEW

I. DESCRIPTION

- Provides system utilization activities, including:
  — Start and stop time
  — Media used
  — Change activity

II. OBJECTIVE

- Provide documentation and historical information, including:
  — Job runs
  — Test descriptions
  — Error tracking

III. ORGANIZATION

- Refer to Systems Librarians (1.2.1), Computer Operators (1.3.1.2), and Job Schedulers (1.3.2.1) in the Organization and Responsibilities Chart

IV. SCHEDULE

- Refer to the Code and Test (6.0), Verification/Validation (7.0), Integration (8.0), Conversion (9.0), Installation and Implementation (10.0), Maintenance (11.0), and Enhancements (12.0) phases and the Data Center—Operations (13.0) section of the Software Life Cycle Chart

SYSTEM UTILIZATION LOG FORM

DATE: January 21, 19XX

OPERATOR: H. Smythe

SYSTEM DESCRIPTION: Salary as reflected by current labor rate plus vacation accumulated plus sick leave accumulated

SYSTEM IDENTIFICATION: salary

JOB IDENTIFICATION	START TIME	STOP TIME
111XXX	1300	1500

CHANGE ACTIVITY DESCRIPTION	TEST DESCRIPTION
isolate & correct database interface code	database integration

MEDIA TYPE	COMMENTS
magnetic tape	database error accessing sick leave

SYSTEM UTILIZATION LOG FORM

DATE:

OPERATOR:

SYSTEM DESCRIPTION:

SYSTEM IDENTIFICATION:

JOB IDENTIFICATION   START TIME   STOP TIME

CHANGE ACTIVITY DESCRIPTION   TEST DESCRIPTION

MEDIA TYPE   COMMENTS

MACHINE-RUN LOG FORM OVERVIEW

I. DESCRIPTION

- Provides machine-run activities, including:
  — Start and stop time
  — Media used
  — Change activity
  — Program custodian

II. OBJECTIVE

- Document historical information, including:
  — Job runs
  — Run classification
  — Software identification

III. ORGANIZATION

- Refer to Systems Librarians (1.2.1), Computer Operators (1.3.1.2), and Job Schedulers (1.3.2.1) in the Organization and Responsibilities Chart

IV. SCHEDULE

- Refer to the Code and Test (6.0), Verification/Validation (7.0), Integration (8.0), Conversion (9.0), Installation and Implementation (10.0), Maintenance (11.0), and Enhancements (12.0) phases and the Data Center—Operations (13.0) section of the Software Life Cycle Chart

MACHINE-RUN LOG FORM

DATE: January 10, 19XX

OPERATOR NAME
M. Johnson

JOB IDENTIFICATION
XXXabc

CLASSIFICATION
Software integration test

ORGANIZATION
Technical support

SOFTWARE NAME
Salary

SOFTWARE IDENTIFICATION
XXXsal

START TIME
1100

STOP TIME
1250

COMMENTS
Performance too slow

MACHINE-RUN LOG FORM

DATE:

OPERATOR NAME   JOB IDENTIFICATION   CLASSIFICATION

ORGANIZATION   SOFTWARE NAME   SOFTWARE IDENTIFICATION

START TIME   STOP TIME   COMMENTS

SYSTEM INCIDENCE LOG FORM OVERVIEW

I. DESCRIPTION

- Provides system incidence activities, including:
  — Start and stop time
  — Program identification
  — Action assignments

II. OBJECTIVE

- Provide documentation and historical information, including:
  — Job runs
  — Incident description
  — Diagnostics

III. ORGANIZATION

- Refer to Systems Librarians (1.2.1), Computer Operators (1.3.1.2), and Job Schedulers (1.3.2.1) in the Organization and Responsibilities Chart

IV. SCHEDULE

- Refer to the Code and Test (6.0), Verification/Validation (7.0), Integration (8.0), Conversion (9.0), Installation and Implementation (10.0), Maintenance (11.0), and Enhancements (12.0) phases and the Data Center—Operations (13.0) section of the Software Life Cycle Chart

SYSTEM INCIDENCE LOG FORM

DATE: July 10, 19XX

OPERATOR NAME	START TIME	STOP TIME	STOP – START TIME
J. Egar	900	1150	250

JOB IDENTIFICATION	PROGRAM IDENTIFICATION	PROGRAM DESCRIPTION
222XXX	Travel	Travel authorization

INCIDENT DESCRIPTION	DIAGNOSTICS	ACTION BY
Does not allocate daily expense reimbursement	Dump does not print this field	I. Gufly

REMARKS
Database requires security access at lower level

SYSTEM INCIDENCE LOG FORM

DATE:

<u>OPERATOR NAME</u>   <u>START TIME</u>   <u>STOP TIME</u>   <u>STOP – START TIME</u>

<u>JOB IDENTIFICATION</u> <u>PROGRAM IDENTIFICATION</u> <u>PROGRAM DESCRIPTION</u>

<u>INCIDENT DESCRIPTION</u>   <u>DIAGNOSTICS</u>   <u>ACTION BY</u>

<u>REMARKS</u>

SOFTWARE PROGRAM REQUIREMENT LOG FORM OVERVIEW

I. DESCRIPTION

- Provides documented history when the software program is input, including:
  — Handling
  — Processing
  — Control of requirements

II. OBJECTIVE

- Ensure that control is maintained, software packages are complete, and revisions have been processed (as either in-work, complete, delinquent, or deferred)
- Track program anomalies
- Provide audit trail

III. ORGANIZATION

- Refer to Systems Librarians (1.2.1), Tape/Disk Librarians (1.3.1.1), Computer Operators (1.3.1.2), and Job Schedulers (1.3.2.1) in the Organization and Responsibility Chart

IV. SCHEDULE

- Refer to the Code and Test (6.0), Verification/Validation (7.0), Integration (8.0), Conversion (9.0), Installation and Implementation (10.0), Maintenance (11.0), and Enhancements (12.0) phases and the Data Center—Operations (13.0) section of Software Life Cycle Chart

SOFTWARE PROGRAM REQUIREMENT LOG FORM

DATE: March 10, 19XX

JOB IDENTIFICATION: HXXZZ

ORIGINATOR: L. Clefe

PHONE #: XXX-1234

SOFTWARE IDENTIFICATION: XXX818

SOFTWARE DESCRIPTION: Business Travel Expense

SOFTWARE ALIAS: BUSTRVL

PRIORITY: 2

DEVICE: 9 Track Tape

DEVICE IDENTIFICATION: XXXA25

SYSTEM NAME: P-50

MODE: Production

VOLUME #: 2

TAPE #: 1

DATA SET IDENTIFICATION: TAUTH55

DATA SET NAME: TRAVEL

INSTRUCTIONS: Generate travel expense forecast

SPECIAL REQUEST: None

OPERATOR NAME: C. Woole

OPERATOR COMMENTS: None

ORIGINATOR COMMENTS: None

SOFTWARE PROGRAM REQUIREMENT LOG FORM

DATE:

JOB IDENTIFICATION:

ORIGINATOR:

PHONE #:

SOFTWARE IDENTIFICATION:

SOFTWARE DESCRIPTION:

SOFTWARE ALIAS:

PRIORITY:

DEVICE:

DEVICE IDENTIFICATION:

SYSTEM NAME:

MODE:

VOLUME #:

TAPE #:

DATA SET IDENTIFICATION:

DATA SET NAME:

INSTRUCTIONS:

SPECIAL REQUEST:

OPERATOR NAME:

OPERATOR COMMENTS:

ORIGINATOR COMMENTS:

SOFTWARE PROGRAM DISTRIBUTION FORM OVERVIEW

I. DESCRIPTION

- Identifies the distribution list
- Maintains control
- Performs archiving

II. OBJECTIVES

- Provide instructions and information when software program is input, including:
  — Handling
  — Processing
  — Control of requirements

III. ORGANIZATION

- Refer to Systems Librarians (1.2.1), Tape/Disk Librarians (1.3.1.1), Computer Operators (1.3.1.2), and Distribution Clerks (1.3.4.1) in the Organization and Responsibilities Chart

IV. SCHEDULE

- Refer to the Code and Test (6.0), Verification/Validation (7.0), Integration (8.0), Conversion (9.0), Installation and Implementation (10.0), Maintenance (11.0), and Enhancements (12.0) phases and the Data Center—Operations (13.0) section of the Software Life Cycle Chart

SOFTWARE PROGRAM DISTRIBUTION FORM

DATE: April 5, 19XX

JOB IDENTIFICATION: HXZXZ

SOFTWARE DESCRIPTION: Business Travel Expense

SOFTWARE ALIAS: BUSTRVL

DATA SET IDENTIFICATION: TAUTH83

DATA SET NAME: TRAVEL-DOMESTIC

RELEASE DATE: March 28, 19XX

OUTPUT DISPOSITION: Approved Production Copy

TAPE DISPOSITION: Archive-3

REFERENCES: EXPENSE

COORDINATOR: L. Clefe

OF COPIES: 3

DISTRIBUTION LIST:

NAME	LOCATION	ORGANIZATION	PHONE	COPY #
H. Bay	3-50	System Engineering	X-1983	1XXX
M. Pim	3-52	Maintenance	X-1521	2XXX
B. Niz	2-29	Software Engineering	X-1223	3XXX

SPECIAL INSTRUCTIONS: None

OPERATOR COMMENTS: None

COORDINATOR COMMENTS: None

SOFTWARE PROGRAM DISTRIBUTION FORM

DATE:

JOB IDENTIFICATION:

SOFTWARE DESCRIPTION:

SOFTWARE ALIAS:

DATA SET IDENTIFICATION:

DATA SET NAME:

RELEASE DATE:

OUTPUT DISPOSITION:

TAPE DISPOSITION:

REFERENCES:

COORDINATOR:

OF COPIES:

DISTRIBUTION LIST:

NAME	LOCATION	ORGANIZATION	PHONE	COPY #

SPECIAL INSTRUCTIONS:

OPERATOR COMMENTS:

COORDINATOR COMMENTS:

DATA CENTER—OPERATION CHECKLIST OVERVIEW

I. DESCRIPTION

• Establishes data center procedures

II. OBJECTIVE

• Ensure software, hardware, networking, and administrative items have been identified, installed, and are functioning properly

III. ORGANIZATION

• Refer to Supervisor of Computer Operations (1.3.1), and Project Manager (1.6) in the Organization and Responsibilities Chart

IV. SCHEDULE

• Refer to the Specifications (4.0), Design (5.0), Code and Test (6.0), Verification/Validation (7.0), Integration (8.0), Conversion (9.0), and Installation and Implementation (10.0) phases and the Data Center— Operations (13.0) section of the Software Life Cycle Chart

DATA CENTER—OPERATIONS CHECKLIST

I. Establish and document data center procedures, including:
- ☐ Software maintenance
- ☐ Hardware maintenance
- ☐ Network maintenance
- ☐ Cable maintenance
- ☐ Disaster/recovery, such as:
    - ☐ Software
    - ☐ Hardware
    - ☐ Networks
    - ☐ Heating
    - ☐ Ventilation
    - ☐ Air conditioning
- ☐ Administrative operations
- ☐ Special operations

II. Ensure proper installation and functioning, including:
- ☐ Software
- ☐ Hardware
- ☐ Networks
- ☐ Cables
- ☐ Heating
- ☐ Ventilation
- ☐ Air conditioning

III. Establish dedicated support, including:
- ☐ Available technical support group
- ☐ Single phone number troubleshooting hotline
- ☐ Hotline hours for customer support

Chapter 14

Security

AUDIT PLAN OVERVIEW

I. DESCRIPTION

* Describes audits planned for existing and new computing systems and processing facilities

II. OBJECTIVES

* Identify systems and facilities to review
* Ensure compliance with corporate objectives and standards regarding security
* Reduce oversight of vulnerabilities of systems and facilities

III. ORGANIZATION

* Refer to MIS Director (1.0), Manager of Development (1.1), Supervisor of Analysis (1.1.1), Supervisor of Design (1.1.2), Supervisor of Programming (1.1.3), Manager of Technical Support (1.2), Computing Auditors (1.2.8), and Supervisor of Computer Operations (1.3.1) in the Organization and Responsibilities Chart

IV. SCHEDULE

* Refer to the Security (14.0) section of the Software Life Cycle Chart

AUDIT PLAN

I. Present title page, which includes:
   A. Document title
   B. Document number
   C. Original release date
   D. Current release date
   E. Current revision number
   F. Appropriate signatures and date

II. Present modifications sheet, which includes:
   A. Sequentially numbered list of changes
   B. Explanation of changes
   C. Page numbers of changes
   D. Appropriate signatures and date

III. Present table of contents, which includes:
   A. Section headings
   B. Chapter titles
   C. Chapter subtitles
   D. Relevant page numbers

IV. Present executive summary, which includes:
   A. Overview
   B. Principal points

V. Present introduction, which includes:
   A. Goals
   B. Scope
   C. Objectives, like:
      • Technical
      • Business
   D. Background information

VI. Describe new security review plan, which includes:
  A. Present current and new systems development overview
  B. Describe controls, including:
      • General
      • Input
      • Processing
      • Output
  C. List standards/procedures
  D. Prepare risk analysis
  E. List selected development projects, including:
      • Audit schedule
      • Audit type
      • Audit resources
      • Audit budget

VII. Describe existing systems, which includes:
  A. Present existing systems overview
  B. Describe controls, including:
      • General
      • Input
      • Processing
      • Output
  C. List standards and procedures
  D. Prepare risk analysis
  E. List selected existing systems, including:
      • Audit schedule
      • Audit type
      • Audit resources
      • Audit budget

VIII. Describe computer centers' security review plan, which includes:
   A. Present facilities overview
   B. Describe controls, including:
      - Data
      - Hiring practices
      - Training
      - Handling violations
      - Contingency planning
   C. List standards and procedures
   D. Prepare risk analysis
   E. List selected facilities, including:
      - Audit schedule
      - Audit type
      - Audit resources
      - Audit budget

IX. Prepare glossary

X. Attach appendixes

COMPUTING FACILITY CONTROLS CHECKLIST OVERVIEW

I. DESCRIPTION

- Details those items that must be secure in a data processing facility, such as a data center or a system library

II. OBJECTIVES

- Help ensure no control weaknesses exist at a facility
- Provide a systematic way to identify whether weaknesses do exist
- Provide visibility for making corrections to any control weaknesses

III. ORGANIZATION

- Refer to Computing Auditors (1.2.8) in the Organization and Responsibilities Chart

IV. SCHEDULE

- Refer to the Security (14.0) section of the Software Life Cycle Chart

COMPUTING FACILITY CONTROLS CHECKLIST

I. Identify or develop personnel controls, regarding:
- ☐ Hiring
- ☐ Termination
- ☐ Separation of duties
- ☐ Job descriptions
- ☐ Organization
- ☐ Shifts
- ☐ Training

II. Identify or develop input controls, regarding:
- ☐ Authorizations
- ☐ Verification
- ☐ Error handling
- ☐ Receipt
- ☐ Passwords
- ☐ Access restrictions, such as:
  - ☐ Data
  - ☐ Programs
  - ☐ Hardware
- ☐ Conversion
- ☐ Data entry
- ☐ Audit trail

III. Identify or develop processing controls, regarding:
- ☐ Job schedules
- ☐ Job priorities
- ☐ Error handling
- ☐ Backup and recovery
- ☐ Deviations
- ☐ Audit trail

IV. Identify or develop output controls, regarding:
- ☐ Distribution
- ☐ Receipt
- ☐ Reports
- ☐ Audit trail

V. Identify or develop documentation controls, regarding:
- ☐ User manuals
- ☐ Operations manuals
- ☐ Logs

VI. Identify or develop administrative controls, regarding:
- ☐ Library procedures
- ☐ Emergency maintenance
- ☐ Moving from test to production
- ☐ Approvals
- ☐ Physical security
- ☐ Security violations and reporting
- ☐ Contingency planning

SYSTEM ACCESS CONTROLS CHECKLIST OVERVIEW

I. DESCRIPTION

- Provides a listing of items to check so that no control problems exist with using the hardware or software of a computing system

II. OBJECTIVES

- Reduce the opportunity for tampering with software, hardware, and data
- Avoid violation of any privacy laws
- Identify any corrective measures to preclude future unauthorized access to a computing system

III. ORGANIZATION

- Refer to Computing Auditors (1.2.8) in the Organization and Responsibilities Chart

IV. SCHEDULE

- Refer to the Requirements (2.0), Verification/Validation (7.0), Maintenance (11.0), and Enhancements (12.0) phases and the Security (14.0) section of the Software Life Cycle Chart

SYSTEM ACCESS CONTROLS CHECKLIST (DEVELOPMENT)

I. Project management controls, including
    A. Identify planning controls, regarding:

- ☐ Schedules
- ☐ Work breakdown structures
- ☐ Time estimates
- ☐ Cost estimates
- ☐ Statement of work
- ☐ Contingency planning
- ☐ Risk assessment
- ☐ Product description

    B. Identify organizing controls, regarding:

- ☐ Responsibilities
- ☐ Meetings
- ☐ Forms
- ☐ Procedures and directives
- ☐ Resource requirements
- ☐ Resource assignments
- ☐ Skill requirements
- ☐ Training
- ☐ Performance standards
- ☐ Organization chart
- ☐ Job descriptions
- ☐ Approvals

C. Identify controls, regarding:

- ☐ Schedule reports
- ☐ Budget reports
- ☐ Resource usage reports
- ☐ Problem reports
- ☐ Change control
- ☐ Reviews
- ☐ Configuration management
- ☐ Quality assurance

II. Life cycle deliverables and documentation, including:
- ☐ Feasibility Study Document
- ☐ Requirements Definition Document
- ☐ Alternatives Analysis Document
- ☐ Preliminary Design Document
- ☐ Detail Design Document
- ☐ Verification/Validation Plan
- ☐ Installation and Implementation Plan
- ☐ User Manual
- ☐ Computer Operator Manual

SYSTEM ACCESS CONTROLS CHECKLIST (SUSTAINING)

I. Administrative controls, including
   A. Identify change control procedures, regarding:
      - ☐ Logging
      - ☐ Evaluation
      - ☐ Moving from test to production
      - ☐ Tracking
      - ☐ Reports

   B. Identify responsibilities, regarding:
      - ☐ Separation of duties
      - ☐ Job descriptions

   C. Identify standards, policies, and procedures, regarding:
      - ☐ Input
      - ☐ Processing
      - ☐ Controls
      - ☐ Error handling

   D. Identify documentation, regarding:
      - ☐ Programs
      - ☐ Databases
      - ☐ Manuals
      - ☐ Reports

   E. Identify maintenance procedures, regarding:
      - ☐ Routine behavior
      - ☐ Emergency behavior

   F. Categorize applications into:
      - ☐ Critical
      - ☐ Noncritical

   G. Identify project management, regarding:
      - ☐ Scheduling
      - ☐ Budgeting
      - ☐ Tracking/monitoring

II. Technical controls, including
  A. Identify input controls, regarding:
    ☐ Authorizations
    ☐ Passwords
    ☐ Edits
    ☐ Error listings and handling
    ☐ Verification
    ☐ Responsibilities
    ☐ Corrective action
    ☐ Reporting
    ☐ Documentation
    ☐ Audit trail
    ☐ Source document handling
    ☐ Data conversion procedures
    ☐ Data storage

  B. Identify processing controls, regarding:
    ☐ Validation and editing
    ☐ File alteration
    ☐ File conversion
    ☐ Responsibilities
    ☐ Exception reports
    ☐ System software
    ☐ Applications
    ☐ Database access
    ☐ Documentation
    ☐ Audit trail
    ☐ Backup and recovery
    ☐ Batch and online processing
    ☐ Error listings and handling
    ☐ Data storage

  C. Identify output controls, regarding:
    ☐ Distribution procedures
    ☐ Reports
    ☐ Responsibilities
    ☐ Documentation
    ☐ Audit trail
    ☐ Balancing and reconciliation
    ☐ Records retention
    ☐ Error handling

Chapter 15

Documentation

USER MANUAL OVERVIEW

I. DESCRIPTION

- Instructions, illustrations, charts, and other documentation on the use of a computer, including hardware and software

II. OBJECTIVES

- Enhance productivity by providing answers to queries about systems
- Give information on how to use a system effectively

III. ORGANIZATION

- Refer to Systems Analysts (1.1.1.2), Methods Analysts (1.1.1.3), Technical Writers (1.2.2), Data Entry Operators (1.3.3.1), Systems Programmers (1.4.2.1), Application Programmers (1.4.2.2), and Project Manager (1.6) in the Organization and Responsibilities Chart

IV. SCHEDULE

- Refer to the Documentation (15.0) section of the Software Life Cycle Chart

USER MANUAL

I. Present title page

II. Prepare introduction, which includes:
   A. Uses
   B. Audience
   C. Distribution
   D. Updates

III. Present table of contents

IV. Present table of illustrations

V. Describe topics, which include:
   A. Functionality, like:
      1. Inputs, such as:
         - Requirements
         - Screens
      2. Processing, such as:
         - Functions
         - Purpose
         - Screens
      3. Outputs, such as:
         - Editing
         - Errors
         - Screens
         - Hardcopy
         - Examples
   B. Databases, like:
      1. File query
      2. System tables
      3. Retention
      4. Backup
      5. Recovery

C. Production schedules
D. Procedures
E. Keys and commands
F. Controls

VI. Prepare glossary

VII. Attach appendixes

DESK PROCEDURES OVERVIEW

I. DESCRIPTION

- Document details on conducting administrative actions

II. OBJECTIVES

- Improve communication
- Reduce duplication of effort
- Build accountability
- Maintain consistency of action

III. ORGANIZATION

- Refer to Systems Analysts (1.1.1.2, 1.4.1.2), Methods Analysts (1.1.1.3, 1.4.1.3), Technical Writers (1.2.2), and Distribution Clerks (1.3.4.1) in the Organization and Responsibilities Chart

IV. SCHEDULE

- Refer to the Documentation (15.0) section of the Software Life Cycle Chart

DESK PROCEDURES

   I. Prepare introduction, which includes:
- A. Purpose
- B. Scope
- C. Objectives
- D. Review date
- E. Signature approvals
- F. References

  II. Describe contents, which include:
- A. Actions, like:
  - Operations
  - Processes
  - Steps
  - Tasks
  - Subtasks
- B. Actors
- C. Illustrations, like:
  - Forms
  - Charts
  - Tables
  - Checklists

III. Prepare glossary

IV. Attach appendixes

COMPUTER OPERATOR MANUAL OVERVIEW

I. DESCRIPTION

- Gives instructions on the use and operation of a computer, including hardware and software

II. OBJECTIVES

- Help overcome learning curves
- Improve understanding of how a system works
- Reduce the effects of employee turnover
- Minimize nonproductive efforts to find answers to queries

III. ORGANIZATION

- Refer to Systems Analysts (1.1.1.2, 1.4.1.2), Methods Analysts (1.1.1.3, 1.4.1.3), Technical Writers (1.2.2), Computer Operators (1.3.1.2), Data Entry Operators (1.3.3.1), and Project Manager (1.6) in the Organization and Responsibilities Chart

IV. SCHEDULE

- Refer to the Documentation (15.0) section of the Software Life Cycle Chart

COMPUTER OPERATOR MANUAL

I. Present table of contents

II. Prepare introduction, which includes:
   - A. Description of manual
   - B. Use of manual
   - C. Updates to manual
   - D. Structure

III. Give system description, which includes:
   - A. Hardware, like:
     - Input
     - Processing
     - Output
   - B. Software, like:
     - Application
     - System
   - C. Data, like:
     - Input
     - Process
     - Files
     - File structure
     - Usage
   - D. Interfaces
   - E. Functions, like:
     - Description
     - Logic
   - F. Capabilities
   - G. Limitations
   - H. System logic

IV. Describe operations, which include:
   A. Jobs, like:
      - Description
      - Priority
      - Schedule
      - Sequence
   B. Manual activities, like:
      - Input
      - Processing
      - Output
   C. Automated activities, like:
      - Operator commands and messages
      - Online activities
      - Batch activities

V. Describe nonroutine activities, which include:
   A. Backup and recovery procedures
   B. Remote operations
   C. Error messages and responses
   D. Approvals

VI. Describe special considerations, which include:
   A. Distribution of output
   B. Routing of output

VII. Prepare glossary

VIII. Attach appendixes

Chapter 16

Training

TRAINING PLAN OVERVIEW

I. DESCRIPTION

- Describes the extent and level of training that will occur within the next year

II. OBJECTIVES

- Identify who will conduct the training
- Describe the courses and resources required when the training occurs
- Describe when the training will occur and where
- Describe the objectives that should be achieved

III. ORGANIZATION

- Refer to MIS Director (1.0) and Project Manager (1.6) in the Organization and Responsibilities Chart

IV. SCHEDULE

- Refer to the Training (16.0) section of the Software Life Cycle Chart

TRAINING PLAN

I. Present title page, which includes:
   A. Document title
   B. Document number
   C. Original release date
   D. Current release date
   E. Current revision number
   F. Appropriate signatures and date

II. Present modifications sheet, which includes:
   A. Sequentially numbered list of changes
   B. Explanation of changes
   C. Page numbers of changes
   D. Appropriate signatures and date

III. Present table of contents, which includes:
   A. Section headings
   B. Chapter titles
   C. Chapter subtitles
   D. Relevant page numbers

IV. Present executive summary, which includes:
   A. Overview
   B. Principal points

V. Present introduction, which includes:
   A. Goals
   B. Scope
   C. Objectives, like:
      • Technical
      • Business
   D. Background information

VI. List goals and objectives, which include:
   A. Short-term goals and objectives
   B. Long-term goals and objectives

VII. Describe courses, which include:
  A. Description, like:
    • Length
    • Summary
    • Objectives
  B. Audiences, like:
    • System users
    • Supervisors and managers
    • Systems maintenance and support personnel
  C. Type of training, like:
    • Computer-based
    • Workshop
    • Lecture

VIII. Describe administrative details, which include:
  A. Schedules
  B. Instructors, like:
    • Permanent
    • Contractors
  C. Locations
  D. Resources
    • Manpower
    • Equipment
    • Facilities
    • Supplies
  E. Registration
  F. Feedback

IX. Prepare glossary

X. Attach appendixes

INSTRUCTOR'S GUIDE OVERVIEW

I. DESCRIPTION

- Explains, page-by-page, course material, especially what is in the Student Handout

II. OBJECTIVES

- Improve communication among instructors
- Clarify the meaning of classroom material
- Ensure all course material is covered adequately and consistently
- Obviate the impact of turnover by training personnel

III. ORGANIZATION

- Refer to Training Analysts (1.2.9) and Project Manager (1.6) in the Organization and Responsibilities Chart

IV. SCHEDULE

- Refer to the Training (16.0) section of the Software Life Cycle Chart

INSTRUCTOR'S GUIDE

I. Present title page

II. Give introduction, which includes:
   A. Objectives
   B. Scope
   C. Length and schedule
   D. Resources, like:
       • Personnel
       • Facilities
       • Equipment
       • Supplies
       • Software
       • Books
   E. Setup

III. Describe each module, which includes:
   A. Objectives
   B. Explanations, like:
       • Bullet lists
       • Charts
       • Diagrams
       • Tables
       • Drawings
   C. Answers to exercises
   D. References

IV. Prepare glossary

V. Attach appendixes

STUDENT HANDOUT OVERVIEW

I. DESCRIPTION

- A document training attendees receive that contains copies of viewfoils and reference materials that attendees can use at their workstations

II. OBJECTIVES

- Provide useful reference information
- Clarify topics
- Facilitate training and learning

III. ORGANIZATION

- Refer to Training Analysts (1.2.9) and Project Manager (1.6) in the Organization and Responsibilities Chart

IV. SCHEDULE

- Refer to the Training (16.0) section of the Software Life Cycle Chart

STUDENT HANDOUT

I. Give introduction, which includes:
  A. Purpose
  B. Scope
  C. Objectives
  D. Prerequisites
  E. Length
  F. Supplies

II. Present table of contents

III. Present table of illustrations

IV. Describe topics (per module), which include:
  A. Objectives
  B. Material, like:
    • Checklists
    • Bullet lists
    • Diagrams
    • Charts
    • Other illustrations
    • Exercises

V. Present case study

VI. Prepare glossary

VII. Attach appendixes

TRAINING SCHEDULE FORM OVERVIEW

I. DESCRIPTION

- A document, typically part of a training plan, that lists or shows when courses will occur, the resources needed to conduct them, the instructors with the requisite skills, and the location of the training

II. OBJECTIVES

- Improve communication among staff members responsible for training
- Facilitate coordination among them

III. ORGANIZATION

- Refer to Training Analysts (1.2.9) and Project Manager (1.6) in the Organization and Responsibilities Chart

IV. SCHEDULE

- Refer to the Training (16.0) section of the Software Life Cycle Chart

TRAINING SCHEDULE FORM

COURSE TITLE	LOCATION	INSTRUCTOR	TIME	HOURS	START DATE	COMPLETION DATE
Data Modeling	Building 55	Rogers	8 a.m.	40	3/19/9X	3/23/9X

TRAINING SCHEDULE FORM

COURSE TITLE	LOCATION	INSTRUCTOR	TIME	HOURS	START DATE	COMPLETION DATE

SECTION IV
ADMINISTRATIVE

Chapter 17

Configuration Management

CONFIGURATION MANAGEMENT PLAN OVERVIEW

I. DESCRIPTION

- Provides guidelines for managing software documentation and distribution, including release and change activities

II. OBJECTIVE

- Establish rigorous treatment of structured methodology before additional configured items and complexities become applicable

III. ORGANIZATION

- Refer to Manager of Development (1.1), Manager of Technical Support (1.2), Configuration Management Specialists (1.2.4), and Project Manager (1.6) in the Organization and Responsibilities Chart

IV. SCHEDULE

- Refer to the Specifications (4.0), Design (5.0), Code and Test (6.0), Verification/Validation (7.0), Integration (8.0), and Conversion (9.0) phases and the Configuration Management (17.0) section of the Software Life Cycle Chart

CONFIGURATION MANAGEMENT PLAN

I. Present title page, which includes:
   A. Document title
   B. Document number
   C. Original release date
   D. Current release date
   E. Current revision number
   F. Appropriate signatures and date

II. Present modifications sheet, which includes:
   A. Sequentially numbered list of changes
   B. Explanation of changes
   C. Page numbers of changes
   D. Appropriate signatures and date

III. Present table of contents, which includes:
   A. Section headings
   B. Chapter titles
   C. Chapter subtitles
   D. Relevant page numbers

IV. Present executive summary, which includes:
   A. Overview
   B. Principal features

V. Present introduction, which includes:
   A. Goals
   B. Scope
   C. Objectives, like:
      • Technical
      • Business
   D. Background information

VI. Identify rigorous treatment for processing and documenting configured releases and change activities, which include:
   A. Mechanisms available and in use
   B. Mechanisms for development procedures in use
   C. Mechanisms for implementation procedures in use
   D. Consistency of electronic media and hardcopy

VII. Identify and resolve change activity impact areas, which include:
   A. Quality
   B. Safety
   C. Schedule
   D. Budget and pricing
   E. Requirements
   F. Specifications
   G. Design
   H. Documentation
   I. Vendor and supplier contracts
   J. Training
   K. Testing
   L. Performance
   M. Reliability
   N. Maintenance
   O. Hardware
   P. Software
   Q. Networking
   R. Interfaces
   S. Baselines
   T. Facilities and storage
   U. Special equipment
   V. Installation
   W. Personnel and organization
   X. Media (magnetic tape, disks, etc.)
   Y. Configuration change
   Z. Engineering and technical
   AA. Business processes
   BB. Remote sites
   CC. Data management
   DD. Database management

VIII. Identify operational requirements, which include:
      A. Costs
      B. Schedules
      C. Personnel
      D. Equipment
      E. Software
      F. Supplies
      G. Facilities and storage

IX. Prepare glossary

X. Attach appendixes

SOFTWARE VERSION FORM OVERVIEW

I. DESCRIPTION

- Reflects most current configuration of each software version, including:
  — Preparation
  — Installation
  — Release

II. OBJECTIVE

- Build a history file for each released configured item

III. ORGANIZATION

- Refer to Supervisor of Programming (1.1.3, 1.4.2), Systems Programmers (1.1.3.1, 1.3.2.2, 1.4.2.1), Application Programmers (1.1.3.2, 1.4.2.2), Manager of Technical Support (1.2), Configuration Management Specialists (1.2.4), Quality-Assurance Specialists (1.2.5), and Testers (1.2.7) in the Organization and Responsibilities Chart

IV. SCHEDULE

- Refer to the Verification/Validation (7.0), Integration (8.0), Conversion (9.0), Installation and Implementation (10.0), Maintenance (11.0), and Enhancements (12.0) phases and the Configuration Management (17.0) section of the Software Life Cycle Chart

SOFTWARE VERSION FORM

IDENTIFICATION: Wklyrpt

PREPARATION NOTICE: 1   REVISION #: 1   DATE: 01/05/XX   BASELINE ID: D

INSTALLATION NOTICE: REVISION #:   DATE: BASELINE ID:

RELEASE NOTICE: REVISION #:   DATE: BASELINE ID:

ABBREVIATIONS/ALIASES: Wkr

NEXT UPPER-LEVEL IDENTIFICATION CODE: Mthr

BRIEF DESCRIPTION: Generates the weekly payroll report

CONSTRAINTS: Automatically dates the report but only recognizes years
beginning with 19, e.g., 19XX

SECURITY RESTRICTIONS: None

INTERFACES: Payroll master

COMPUTING SYSTEM: Abc system 10XX

PERIPHERALS: Def Printer, model 20YY

REMARKS: Constraint will cause major impact if not resolved before end of 1999

MEDIA LOCATION: Bldg 1, Floor 1, Room 1

CONTRACT LABOR COMPANY NAME: QRS Company

CONTRACT LABOR IDENTIFICATION: QRS-ZZZ

APPROVALS/DATE:

Lou Kant 12/10/XX PROGRAMMER	Emma Good 12/15/XX SUPERVISOR OF PROGRAMMING
Hui Testum 12/19/XX TESTER	Mark Canicol 12/21/XX QUALITY-ASSURANCE SPECIALIST
Irv Chartum 12/23/XX MANAGER OF TECHNICAL SUPPORT	Rita Face 12/29/XX CONFIGURATION MANAGEMENT SPECIALIST

SOFTWARE VERSION FORM

IDENTIFICATION:

PREPARATION NOTICE: 1   REVISION #:   DATE: BASELINE ID:

INSTALLATION NOTICE: REVISION #:   DATE: BASELINE ID:

RELEASE NOTICE: REVISION #:   DATE: BASELINE ID:

ABBREVIATIONS/ALIASES:

NEXT UPPER-LEVEL IDENTIFICATION CODE:

BRIEF DESCRIPTION:

CONSTRAINTS:

SECURITY RESTRICTIONS:

INTERFACES:

COMPUTING SYSTEM:

PERIPHERALS:

REMARKS:

MEDIA LOCATION:

CONTRACT LABOR COMPANY NAME:

CONTRACT LABOR IDENTIFICATION:

APPROVALS/DATE:

_____   _____
PROGRAMMER   SUPERVISOR OF PROGRAMMING

_____   _____
TESTER   QUALITY-ASSURANCE SPECIALIST

_____   _____
MANAGER OF TECHNICAL   CONFIGURATION MANAGEMENT
SUPPORT   SPECIALIST

PROBLEM REPORT FORM AND FLOWCHART OVERVIEW

I. DESCRIPTION

- Identifies problems, requests resolution, and documents software and hardware issues
- This form may be filled out by any organization

II. OBJECTIVE

- Provide formal and consistent process for problem resolution

III. ORGANIZATION

- Refer to Configuration Management Specialists (1.2.4) and Testers (1.2.7) in the Organization and Responsibilities Chart

IV. SCHEDULE

- Refer to the Design (5.0), Code and Test (6.0), Verification/Validation (7.0), Integration (8.0), Conversion (9.0), Installation and Implementation (10.0), Maintenance (11.0), and Enhancements (12.0) phases and the Configuration Management (17.0) section of the Software Life Cycle Chart

PROBLEM REPORT FORM

IDENTIFICATION: Wklyrpt

PROBLEM REPORT#: 1
REFERENCE #: RUMR
CONTRACT #:QRS-20XX

ERROR FIX: N/A

ENHANCEMENT: Yes

DATE SUBMITTED: 06-17-XX

DATE RECEIVED: 06-20-XX

BRIEF DESCRIPTION: Automatically dates the report, but only recognizes years beginning with 19, e.g., 19XX

CHANGE EXPLANATION: Allow the system to use years beginning with 20, e.g., 20YY

AFFECTED INTERFACES: Payroll master

CHANGE IMPLEMENTATION: Revise the code to accommodate years 20XX ff.

SOFTWARE TEST VERIFICATION: Run dummy data through the system to test upgraded software. Run mass extracts and clean up errors.

DOCUMENTATION UPDATED DATE: 10-11-XX

SOFTWARE UPDATED DATE: 10-25-XX

HARDWARE UPDATED DATE:

REMARKS: Must do periodic check to ensure that no 20XX dates can be valid in 19XX years

Signature and Date Block:

Chris Tomitey   06-01-XX
ORIGINATOR

Harry Pasturn   09-27-XX
TESTER

Allen Hokay   10-15-XX
CONFIGURATION MANAGEMENT SPECIALIST

PROBLEM REPORT FORM

IDENTIFICATION: REVISION #:

PROBLEM REPORT#:
REFERENCE #:
CONTRACT #:

ERROR FIX:

ENHANCEMENT:

DATE SUBMITTED:

DATE RECEIVED:

BRIEF DESCRIPTION:

CHANGE EXPLANATION:

AFFECTED INTERFACES:

CHANGE IMPLEMENTATION:

SOFTWARE TEST VERIFICATION:

DOCUMENTATION UPDATED DATE:

SOFTWARE UPDATED DATE:

HARDWARE UPDATED DATE:

REMARKS:

Signature and Date Block:

_____
ORIGINATOR

_____
TESTER

_____
CONFIGURATION MANAGEMENT SPECIALIST

PROBLEM REPORT FLOWCHART

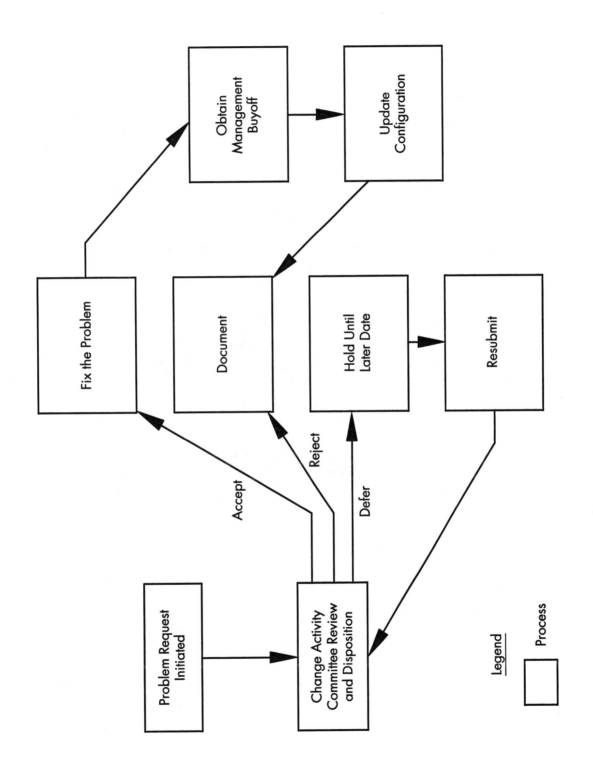

CONFIGURATION AUDIT CHECKLIST OVERVIEW

I. DESCRIPTION

- Ensures that configured items' test results concur with requirements (known as a functional audit)
- Ensures documentation concurs with specifications (known as a physical audit)

II. OBJECTIVES

- Provide functional audit trail
- Provide physical audit trail

III. ORGANIZATION

- Refer to Manager of Technical Support (1.2), Configuration Management Specialists (1.2.4), Quality-Assurance Specialists (1.2.5), Testers (1.2.7), and Computing Auditors (1.2.8) in the Organization and Responsibilities Chart

IV. SCHEDULE

- Refer to the Verification/Validation (7.0), Integration (8.0), Conversion (9.0), and Installation and Implementation (10.0) phases and the Configuration Management (17.0) section of the Software Life Cycle Chart

CONFIGURATION AUDIT CHECKLIST

I. Document configuration items, including:
- ☐ Configured items delivered
- ☐ Configured items verified
- ☐ Documentation matches its representative media
- ☐ Technical documentation is complete and accurate

II. Establish procedures and plans, including:
- ☐ Functional audit plan
- ☐ Physical audit plan
- ☐ Test plans, methods, procedures, and results reviewed for compliance (functional configuration audit)

III. Document audits, reports, and records, including:
- ☐ Functional audit test data and reports verifying that test results concur with requirements
- ☐ Physical audit code and documentation records that agree with the specifications
- ☐ Problem reports are complete, in work, deferred, or delinquent
- ☐ Quality-assurance test records availability and completeness

FILE ARCHIVE FORM OVERVIEW

I. DESCRIPTION

- Identifies the most current file, associated attributes, and release date

II. OBJECTIVE

- Provide archive history

III. ORGANIZATION

- Refer to Tape/Disk Librarians (1.3.1.1) and Configuration Management Specialists (1.2.4) in the Organization and Responsibilities Chart

IV. SCHEDULE

- Refer to the Specifications (4.0), Design (5.0), Code and Test (6.0), Verification/Validation (7.0), Integration (8.0), Conversion (9.0), Installation and Implementation (10.0), Maintenance (11.0), and Enhancements (12.0) phases and the Configuration Management (17.0) section of the Software Life Cycle Chart

FILE ARCHIVE FORM

DATE: 03-05-19XX

FILE NAME: Attendance

FILE NUMBER: 57XX

MEDIA TYPE: Disk cartridge

MEDIA #: 52-F

TAPE/DISK DENSITY: 1 million bytes

OF TRACKS: 200

PHYSICAL BLOCK SIZE: 150 bytes

LOGICAL BLOCK SIZE: 20 bytes

RECORDING MODE: Magnetic disk

CHARACTER CODE: EBCDIC

USER MANUAL REFLECTS CURRENT RELEASE: Yes

BACKUP - LOCATION: Offsite house 1

      - FILENAME: Attend

      - FILE #: 5

      - MEDIUM: Tape

ACCESS RESTRICTIONS: None

VENDOR CONTACT: Ira Dabest

VENDOR PHONE #: 123-XXXX

FILE ARCHIVE FORM

DATE:

FILE NAME:

FILE NUMBER:

MEDIA TYPE:

MEDIA #:

TAPE/DISK DENSITY:

OF TRACKS:

PHYSICAL BLOCK SIZE:

LOGICAL BLOCK SIZE:

RECORDING MODE:

CHARACTER CODE:

USER MANUAL REFLECTS CURRENT RELEASE:

BACKUP - LOCATION:

      - FILENAME:

      - FILE #:

      - MEDIUM:

ACCESS RESTRICTIONS:

VENDOR CONTACT:

VENDOR PHONE #:

FILE REQUEST FORM OVERVIEW

I. DESCRIPTION

- Requests the most current file and associated attributes
- Form can be generated by any organization

II. OBJECTIVE

- Provide access to most current file for review or updates

III. ORGANIZATION

- Refer to Tape/Disk Librarians (1.3.1.1) in the Organization and Responsibilities Chart

IV. SCHEDULE

- Refer to the Specifications (4.0), Design (5.0), Code and Test (6.0), Verification/Validation (7.0), Integration (8.0), Conversion (9.0), Installation and Implementation (10.0), Maintenance (11.0), and Enhancements (12.0) phases and the Configuration Management (17.0) section of the Software Life Cycle Chart

FILE REQUEST FORM

ORIGINATOR: T. Mead
PHONE #: 111-XXXX

RETURN DATE: 09-19-XX
TODAY'S DATE: 08-15-XX

REQUESTED ITEM(S):
Identification: Caldate

Rev #: 3

USED BY/FOR:

TAPE TYPE: Punch

COPY #: 6

DISK TYPE: Cartridge

COPY #: 4

LOCATION: Archive identification 236XX

ACCESS RESTRICTION: None

PURCHASING/PROCUREMENT: P. Grien
PHONE #: 555-XXXX

DATE: 08-13-XX

VENDOR CONTACT: Ira Dabest

VENDOR PHONE#: 123-XXXX

SIGNATURE BLOCK AND DATE:

T. Meade   08-10-XX
Originator

F. Bender   08-12-XX
Tape/Disk Librarian

FILE REQUEST FORM

ORIGINATOR: RETURN DATE:
PHONE #:   TODAY'S DATE:

REQUESTED ITEM(S):
Identification: Rev #:

USED BY/FOR:

TAPE TYPE: COPY #:

DISK TYPE: COPY #:

LOCATION:

ACCESS RESTRICTION:

PURCHASING/PROCUREMENT:

PHONE #:   DATE:

VENDOR CONTACT:

VENDOR PHONE #:

SIGNATURE BLOCK AND DATE:

_____
Originator

_____
Tape/Disk Librarian

PATCH REQUEST FORM OVERVIEW

I. DESCRIPTION

- Provides temporary software fixes until a permanent one(s) can be installed
- A permanent software fix is the only means of closing out a problem report

II. OBJECTIVES

- Reduce waiting time for permanent software fix to be developed, tested, and installed
- Facilitate continuity of work progress

III. ORGANIZATION

- Refer to Supervisor of Programming (1.1.3, 1.4.2), Systems Programmers (1.1.3.1, 1.3.2.2, 1.4.2.1), Application Programmers (1.1.3.2, 1.4.2.2), and Configuration Management Specialists (1.2.4) in the Organization and Responsibilities Chart

IV. SCHEDULE

- Refer to the Code and Test (6.0), Verification/Validation (7.0), Integration (8.0), Conversion (9.0), Installation and Implementation (10.0), Maintenance (11.0), and Enhancements (12.0) phases and the Configuration Management (17.0) section of the Software Life Cycle Chart

PATCH REQUEST FORM

PATCH PROGRAMMER NAME: Peter Petch

DATE: 05-02-XX

CONFIGURATION ITEM NAME (DESCRIPTION): Labcol (labor collection)

VERSION #: 2

VERIFICATION TEST #: 4

PROBLEM REPORT #: 1XX

REVISED INSTRUCTION SET: Modify Code (see Reason for Patch section)

REASON FOR PATCH: Temporary override of duplicate charging

REVISED SECTION: 1XXX-1

OLD SECTION: 1XXX-0

REVISED MEMORY LOCATION: Produ-2x

OLD MEMORY LOCATION: Produ-1x

PATCH REQUEST FORM

PATCH PROGRAMMER NAME:

DATE:

CONFIGURATION ITEM NAME (DESCRIPTION):

VERSION #:

VERIFICATION TEST #:

PROBLEM REPORT #:

REVISED INSTRUCTION SET:

REASON FOR PATCH:

REVISED SECTION:

OLD SECTION:

REVISED MEMORY LOCATION:

OLD MEMORY LOCATION:

Chapter 18

Quality

SOFTWARE QUALITY-ASSURANCE PLAN OVERVIEW

I. DESCRIPTION

- Defines responsibilities and tasks to ensure that application software agrees with project quality standards, including:
  — Development
  — Implementation
  — Maintenance
  — Monitoring
  — Reviews
  — Audits

II. OBJECTIVE

- Integrate quality into the software life cycle through an unbiased independent party

III. ORGANIZATION

- Refer to Manager of Technical Support (1.2), Configuration Management Specialists (1.2.4), Quality-Assurance Specialists (1.2.5), Testers (1.2.7), Computing Auditors (1.2.8), Manager of Sustaining (1.4), and Project Manager (1.6) in the Organization and Responsibilities Chart

IV. SCHEDULE

- Refer to the Specifications (4.0) and Design (5.0) phases and the Quality (18.0) section of the Software Life Cycle Chart

SOFTWARE QUALITY-ASSURANCE PLAN

   I. Present title page, which includes:
- A. Document title
- B. Document number
- C. Original release date
- D. Current release date
- E. Current revision number
- F. Appropriate signatures and date

  II. Present modifications sheet, which includes:
- A. Sequentially numbered list of changes
- B. Explanations of changes
- C. Page numbers of changes
- D. Appropriate signatures and date

 III. Present table of contents, which includes:
- A. Section headings
- B. Chapter titles
- C. Chapter subtitles
- D. Relevant page numbers

 IV. Present executive summary, which includes:
- A. Overview
- B. Principal points

  V. Present introduction, which includes:
- A. Goals
- B. Scope
- C. Objectives, like:
  - Technical
  - Business
- D. Background information

VI. Establish rigorous treatment of compliance and auditing, which includes:
    A. Engineering and technical support procedures, tests, reports, and records
    B. Traceability of requirements (from what was delivered to what was required)

VII. Prepare glossary

VIII. Attach appendixes

MAINTENANCE CONTROL REPORT FORM OVERVIEW

I. DESCRIPTION

- Provides current quality-assurance status of software including:
  - Submittal
  - Documentation
  - Problem resolution
- When software is no longer being used, is sold, or is licensed, then maintenance control is discontinued

II. OBJECTIVE

- Support quality-assurance accreditation of software

III. ORGANIZATION

- Refer to Configuration Management Specialists (1.2.4), Quality-Assurance Specialists (1.2.5), Supervisor of Analysis (1.4.1), and Database Analysts (1.4.1.1) in the Organization and Responsibilities Chart

IV. SCHEDULE

- Refer to the Specifications (4.0), Design (5.0), Code and Test (6.0), Verification/Validation (7.0), Integration (8.0), Conversion (9.0), Installation and Implementation (10.0), Maintenance (11.0), and Enhancements (12.0) phases and the Quality (18.0) section of the Software Life Cycle Chart

MAINTENANCE CONTROL REPORT FORM

DATE: June 10, 19XX

PURPOSE: Support network protocol for upload and download of data

SECTION NAME: Netproto   SECTION #: 1 thru 5

SECTION SUMMARY: Provide user with transparent movement of data

MACHINE: Personal computer # qrs   HOST: Mainframe xyz

SYSTEM SOFTWARE: Mainframe xyz, operating system GHI

HARDWARE CONFIGURATION: Network port in personal computer qrs to
network port in mainframe xyz

INTERFACE MODULES: Control internet protocol

EXTERNAL SYSTEMS: Virteqpt   EXTERNAL MODULES: Netwre3x

DATABASE INTERFACES: Rmasterl, Transl

NETWORK: Network lmn

REQUIREMENTS TRACEABILITY: Yes

FLOW DIAGRAMS
    - MODULE: Netmlxx
    - DATA: Netd2xx

SOFTWARE LANGUAGE: PENIX

OVERLAYS: Overly2x

ERROR MESSAGE RESPONSES: Series 1X protocol error messages

PROGRAM FILES: Netx.net, Nety.net

PROGRAM DOCUMENT #: Net docl-xx   VERSION #: 2.0-X

TEST SAMPLE REPORT #: Net5-x; Net6-x; Net7-x

ERROR REPORTS: 10 to date

PERFORMANCE ACTIVITY: High

PREVENTIVE MAINTENANCE: None   DIAGNOSTICS: None

VENDOR PURCHASED: Yes

MAINTENANCE CONTROL REPORT FORM

DATE:

PURPOSE:

SECTION NAME: SECTION #:

SECTION SUMMARY:

MACHINE: HOST:

SYSTEM SOFTWARE:

HARDWARE CONFIGURATION:

INTERFACE MODULES:

EXTERNAL SYSTEMS: EXTERNAL MODULES:

DATABASE INTERFACES:

NETWORK:

REQUIREMENTS TRACEABILITY:

FLOW DIAGRAMS

SOFTWARE LANGUAGE:

OVERLAYS:

ERROR MESSAGE RESPONSES:

PROGRAM FILES:

PROGRAM DOCUMENT #:   VERSION #:

TEST SAMPLE REPORT #:

ERROR REPORTS:

PERFORMANCE ACTIVITY:

PREVENTIVE MAINTENANCE: DIAGNOSTICS

VENDOR PURCHASED:

QUALITY-CIRCLES PLAN OVERVIEW

I. DESCRIPTION

- Improves productivity for the company by focusing on processes, not people
- Brainstorms divergent thinking process improvements

II. OBJECTIVE

- Improve quality and quality image

III. ORGANIZATION

- Any group of voluntary members focusing on improving quality
- Only nonmanagement personnel participate

IV. SCHEDULE

- Refer to the Maintenance (11.0) and Enhancements (12.0) phases and the Quality (18.0) section of the Software Life Cycle Chart
- Meetings are regularly scheduled in an impartial area (e.g., cafeteria)

QUALITY CIRCLES PLAN

I. Present title page, which includes:
  - A. Document title
  - B. Document number
  - C. Original release date
  - D. Current release date
  - E. Current revision number
  - F. Appropriate signatures and date

II. Present modifications sheet, which includes:
  - A. Sequentially numbered list of changes
  - B. Explanations of changes
  - C. Page numbers of changes
  - D. Appropriate signatures and date

III. Present table of contents, which includes:
  - A. Section headings
  - B. Chapter titles
  - C. Chapter subtitles
  - D. Relevant page numbers

IV. Present executive summary, which includes:
  - A. Overview
  - B. Principal points

V. Present introduction, which includes:
  - A. Goals
  - B. Scope
  - C. Objectives, like:
    - Technical
    - Business
  - D. Background information

VI. Define quality-circle charter, which includes:
   A. Problem identification
   B. Brainstorming
   C. Analysis

VII. Prepare glossary

VIII. Attach appendixes

QUALITY-CIRCLES CHECKLIST OVERVIEW

I. DESCRIPTION

- Provides list of quality-circle opportunities

II. OBJECTIVE

- Summarize functions and operations of quality circles

III. ORGANIZATION

- Any group of voluntary members focusing on improving quality
- Only nonmanagement personnel participate

IV. SCHEDULE

- Refer to the Maintenance (11.0) and Enhancements (12.0) phases and the Quality (18.0) section of the Software Life Cycle Chart
- Meetings are regularly scheduled in an impartial area (e.g., cafeteria)

QUALITY-CIRCLES CHECKLIST

I.   Identify the operational aspects of the quality circle, including:

- ☐ Upper-management commitment
- ☐ Funding to implement the suggestions and recommendations
- ☐ Percentage breakdowns for reductions in labor hours, labor cost, equipment cost, downtime, rework, and scrap
- ☐ Growth opportunities assessment, both strategically and tactically
- ☐ Union participation and involvement

II. Identify the functional aspects of the quality circle, including:

- ☐ Visits to other Quality Circle meetings
- ☐ Training plan for team leader and Circle members
- ☐ Quantitative measurements for improvement factors
- ☐ Ability in dealing with complaints
- ☐ Improved morale, professional, and personal growth for the Circle and its effects on non-Circle members

STATISTICAL QUALITY-CONTROL GRAPHS OVERVIEW

I. DESCRIPTION

- Provides statistical graphs that monitor productivity and quality

- Identify anomalies

- Indicate trending patterns

- Determine when processes are in or out of control regions

- Statistical quality-control graphs definitions:
  - Run Charts are graphical depictions of a variable that a succession of items over time are measured to indicate (increasing or decreasing) trends

  - X Bar Control Charts are displays of the variation in sample averages of a variable

  - R Control Charts are displays of the variation in the sample ranges of a variable

  - Pareto Diagrams are graphical depictions of variables that rank problem and improvement areas

  - Fishbone Diagrams are diagrams of causes and associated effects that provide the framework for data collection and subsequent analysis

  - Histograms are graphical depictions of size, shape, and variation used to statistically analyze a process

  - Flow Charts are charts that provide the logical flow of a process from one point to another; they identify completely the process that lends itself to problem definition (or lack thereof) and isolate high-risk areas

II. OBJECTIVES

- Improve visibility and provide direction for production, output, and quality

III. ORGANIZATION

- Refer to Supervisor of Analysis (1.1.1, 1.4.1), Methods Analysts (1.1.1.3, 1.4.1.3), Manager of Operations (1.3), and Manager of Sustaining (1.4) in the Organization and Responsibilities Chart

IV. SCHEDULE

- Refer to the Maintenance (11.0) and Enhancements (12.0) phases and the Quality (18.0) section of the Software Life Cycle Chart

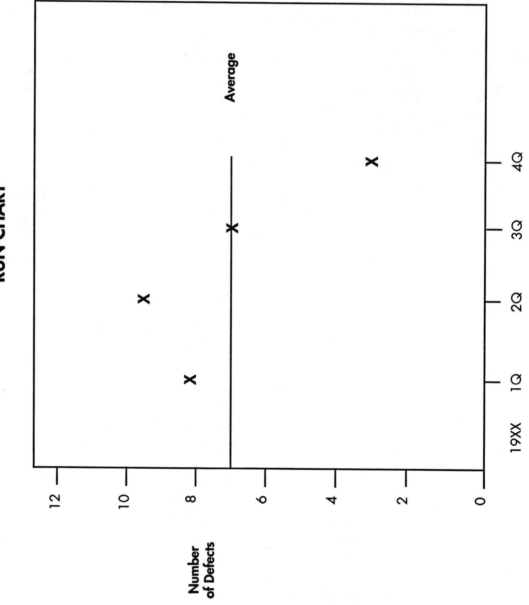

DEFECTS IN PAYROLL SOFTWARE
RUN CHART

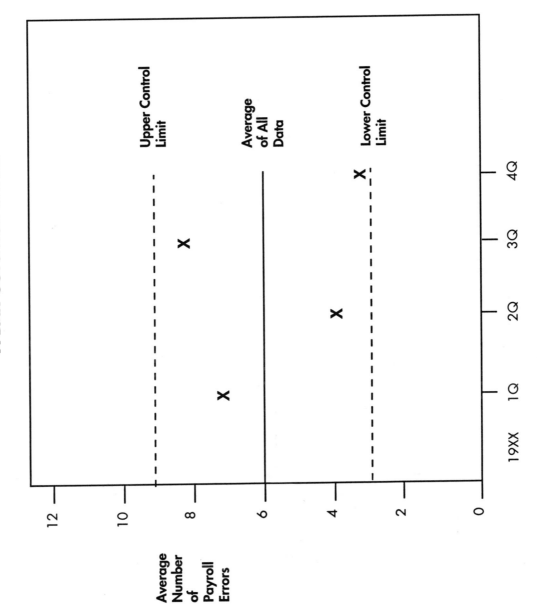

NUMBER OF PAYROLL ERRORS in 19XX
X BAR CONTROL CHART

Upper Control Limit

Average of All Data

Lower Control Limit

Average Number of Payroll Errors

12
10
8
6
4
2
0

19XX   1Q   2Q   3Q   4Q

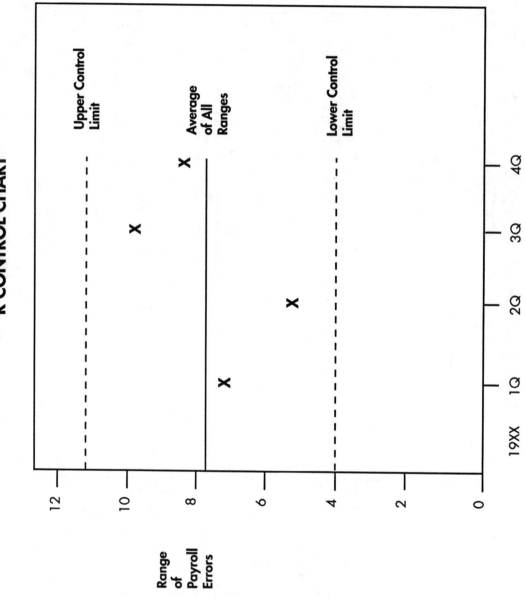

RANGE OF PAYROLL ERRORS IN 19XX
R CONTROL CHART

Upper Control
Limit

Average
of All
Ranges

Lower Control
Limit

19XX   1Q   2Q   3Q   4Q

12

10

8

6

4

2

0

Range
of
Payroll
Errors

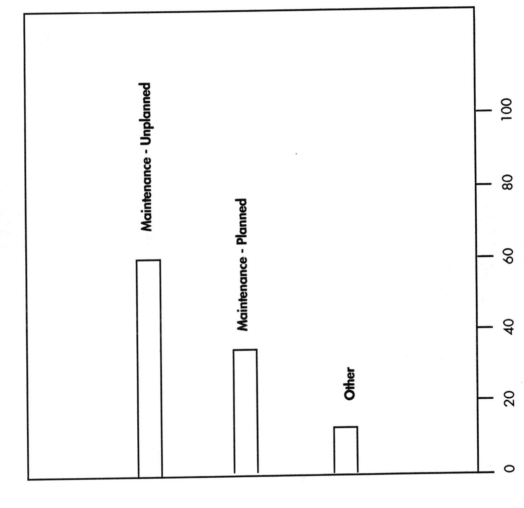

EQUIPMENT DOWNTIME 19XX
PARETO DIAGRAM

Maintenance - Unplanned

Maintenance - Planned

Other

0   20   40   60   80   100

Percentage

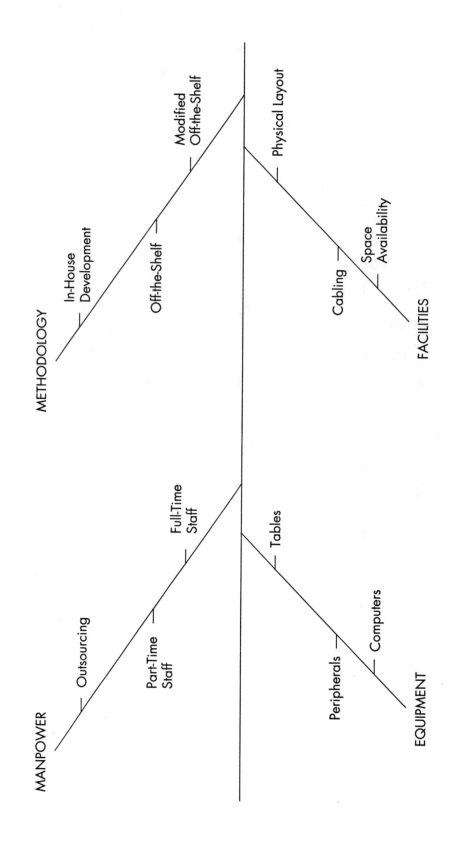

PAYROLL SOFTWARE

FISHBONE DIAGRAM

MANPOWER

Outsourcing

Part-Time
Staff

Full-Time
Staff

METHODOLOGY

In-House
Development

Off-the-Shelf

Modified
Off-the-Shelf

Physical Layout

Cabling

Space
Availability

FACILITIES

Tables

Peripherals

Computers

EQUIPMENT

BENEFITS PAID IN 19XX
HISTOGRAM

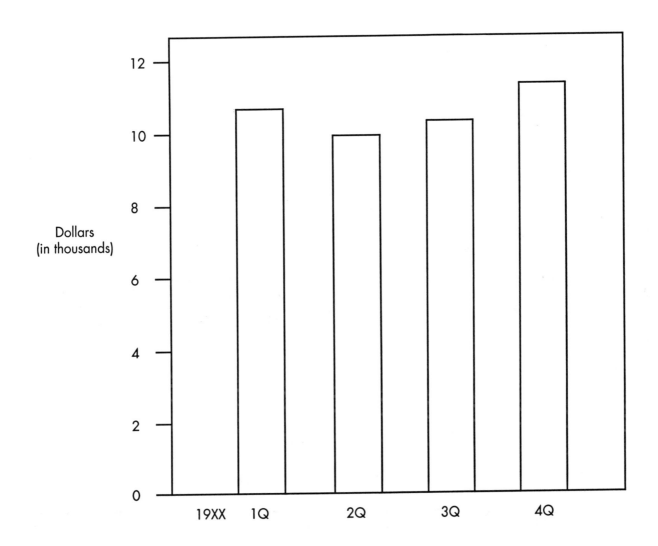

SOFTWARE INSTALLATION FLOWCHART

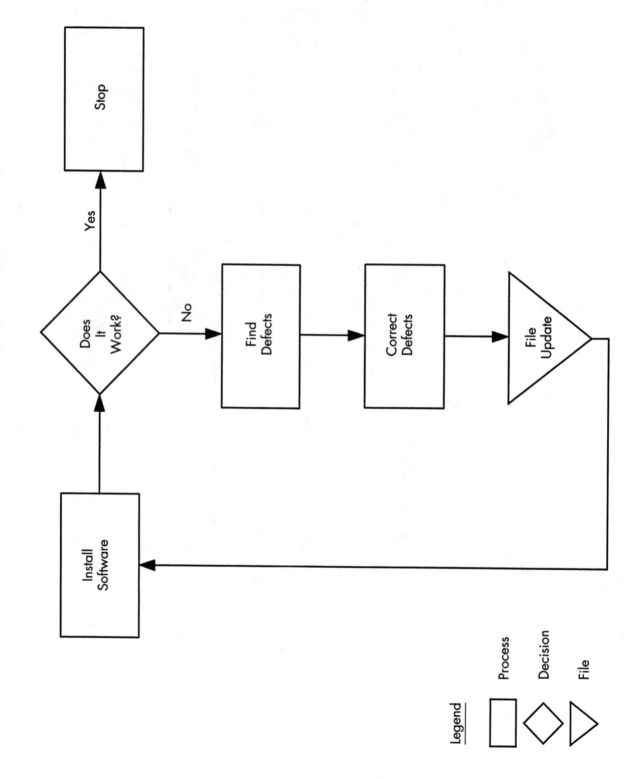

Install Software

Does It Work?

Yes → Stop

No → Find Defects → Correct Defects → File Update

Legend

Process

Decision

File

STATISTICAL QUALITY-CONTROL CHECKLIST OVERVIEW

I. DESCRIPTION

- Defines parameters and evaluation criteria for statistical control

II. OBJECTIVE

- Determine trends (increasing or decreasing) and quality improvement

III. ORGANIZATION

- Refer to Supervisor of Analysis (1.1.1, 1.4.1) and Methods Analysts (1.1.1.3, 1.4.1.3) in the Organization and Responsibilities Chart

IV. SCHEDULE

- Refer to the Maintenance (11.0) and Enhancements (12.0) phases and the Quality (18.0) section of the Software Life Cycle Chart
- The Statistical Quality-Control Checklist is published at regular intervals, (e.g., weekly, monthly, quarterly)

STATISTICAL QUALITY-CONTROL CHECKLIST

Identify appropriate parameters and evaluation criteria, including:

- ☐ Budget
- ☐ Schedule
- ☐ Rework
- ☐ Scrap
- ☐ Customer satisfaction
- ☐ Modified design
- ☐ New design
- ☐ Manpower
- ☐ Inventory stock
- ☐ Facilities accommodations
- ☐ Transportation
- ☐ Sales opportunities
- ☐ Inspections
- ☐ Inventory accuracy
- ☐ Data accessibility
- ☐ Database accessibility
- ☐ Types of control required
- ☐ Maintenance
- ☐ Computer software (optional)
- ☐ Computer hardware (optional)

Chapter 19

Standards

STANDARDS AND GUIDELINES MANUAL OVERVIEW

I. DESCRIPTION

- Compilation of procedures, policies, and reference material that personnel can refer to during the development, maintenance, and operational activities of a data processing department

II. OBJECTIVES

- Provide consistency in organizational activities
- Reduce nonproductive time since "answers" or "guidance" are readily available
- Improve communication among employees in the department

III. ORGANIZATION

- Refer to Systems Analysts (1.1.1.2), Methods Analysts (1.1.1.3, 1.4.1.3), and Technical Writers (1.2.2) in the Organization and Responsibilities Chart

IV. SCHEDULE

- Refer to the Standards (19.0) section of the Software Life Cycle Chart

STANDARDS AND GUIDELINES MANUAL

    I. Present title page

   II. Give introduction, which includes:
        A. Distribution
        B. Uses
        C. Audience
        D. Updates

  III. Present table of contents

  IV. Present table of illustrations

   V. Describe topics, which include:
        A. Operations
        B. Utilities
        C. Data dictionary
        D. Security
        E. Technical services
        F. Programming standards
        G. Data standards
        H. Methodology standards
         I. Training
        J. Project management
        K. Personnel
        L. Documentation

  VI. Prepare glossary

 VII. Attach appendixes

VIII. Add index

DISASTER RECOVERY PLAN OVERVIEW

I. DESCRIPTION

- Details the actions, resources, and priorities to pursue when a disaster, man-made or natural, strikes a data processing department
- Should be definitive enough to enable recovery to "normal" business activities within a short time period

II. OBJECTIVES

- Document the means of recovery under various conditions
- Enhance communications under less than normal circumstances
- Enable a more cost-effective recovery

III. ORGANIZATION

- Refer to Systems Analysts (1.1.1.2, 1.4.1.2) and Methods Analysts (1.1.1.3, 1.4.1.3) in the Organization and Responsibilities Chart

IV. SCHEDULE

- Refer to the Standards (19.0) section of the Software Life Cycle Chart

DISASTER RECOVERY PLAN

I. Present title page, which includes:
   A. Document title
   B. Document number
   C. Original release date
   D. Current release date
   E. Current revision number
   F. Appropriate signatures and date

II. Present modifications sheet, which includes:
   A. Sequentially numbered list of changes
   B. Explanation of changes
   C. Page numbers of changes
   D. Appropriate signatures and date

III. Present table of contents, which includes:
   A. Section headings
   B. Chapter titles
   C. Chapter subtitles
   D. Relevant page numbers

IV. Present executive summary, which includes:
   A. Overview
   B. Principal points

V. Present introduction, which includes:
   A. Goals
   B. Scope
   C. Objectives, like:
      • Technical
      • Business
   D. Background information

VI. Identify disaster recovery team, which includes:
   A. Members
   B. Responsibilities

VII. Define damage assessment, which includes:
- A. Major disaster criteria and corresponding actions
- B. Minor disaster criteria and corresponding actions
- C. Assessment areas, like:
  - Personnel
  - Equipment
  - Supplies
  - Facilities
  - Documentation

VIII. Describe critical operations, which include:
- A. Production scheduling requirements
- B. Processing times

IX. Describe recovery procedures, which include:
- A. Personnel
- B. Equipment
- C. Supplies
- D. Facilities
- E. Documentation
- F. Restart considerations, like:
  - Programs
  - Files

X. Prepare glossary

XI. Attach appendixes

RISK ASSESSMENT CHECKLIST OVERVIEW

I. DESCRIPTION

- Identifies the possible occurrences that can affect the outcome of a project

II. OBJECTIVES

- To develop measures to avoid or offset the occurrence of a negative event
- Encourage proactive, rather than reactive, project management

III. ORGANIZATION

- Refer to Computing Auditors (1.2.8) in the Organization and Responsibilities Chart

IV. SCHEDULE

- Refer to the Standards (19.0) section of the Software Life Cycle Chart

RISK ASSESSMENT CHECKLIST

I. Identify planning risks, related to:
- ☐ Statement of work
- ☐ Work breakdown structure
- ☐ Time estimates
- ☐ Budget estimates
- ☐ Scheduling
- ☐ Product definition
- ☐ Automated project management
- ☐ Project plan
- ☐ Life cycle

II. Identify organizing risks, related to:
- ☐ Task assignments
- ☐ Staffing
- ☐ Training
- ☐ Project handbook
- ☐ Reports
- ☐ Forms
- ☐ Resource allocation, regarding:
  - ☐ People
  - ☐ Hardware
  - ☐ Software
  - ☐ Data
  - ☐ Supplies
  - ☐ Facilities
- ☐ Organization chart
- ☐ Client participation
- ☐ Senior management support

III. Identify controlling risks, related to:
- ☐ Contingency plans
- ☐ Tracking of plans versus actuals, like:
  - ☐ Cost
  - ☐ Schedule
  - ☐ Quality
- ☐ Meetings, like:

- ☐ Status review
- ☐ Checkpoint review
- ☐ Staff
- ☐ Change control
- ☐ Configuration management
- ☐ Quality assurance
- ☐ Milestone benchmarks

IV. Identify technical risks, related to:

- ☐ Testing procedures
- ☐ Development of life cycle deliverables, like:
    - ☐ Feasibility Study Document
    - ☐ Requirements Definition Document
    - ☐ Alternatives Analysis Document
    - ☐ Functional Specifications Document
    - ☐ Preliminary Design Document
    - ☐ Detail Design Document
    - ☐ Verification/Validation Plan
    - ☐ Installation and Implementation Plan
- ☐ Control of data
- ☐ Development tools
- ☐ Development techniques
- ☐ User documentation
- ☐ Product quality
- ☐ Training
- ☐ System security
- ☐ Operations manual
- ☐ Design, regarding:
    - ☐ Programs
    - ☐ Data
    - ☐ Procedures
    - ☐ Security
    - ☐ Documentation

SOFTWARE DOCUMENTATION CHECKLIST OVERVIEW

I. DESCRIPTION

- Provides a listing of all software policies, procedures, manuals, diagrams, illustrations, and specifications required for a data processing organization, such as for a project or department

II. OBJECTIVES

- Identify what should be present in an organization
- Identify who should have which documentation
- Enable better control over documentation

III. ORGANIZATION

- Refer to Systems Analysts (1.1.1.2), Methods Analysts (1.1.1.3), and Technical Writers (1.2.2) in the Organization and Responsibilities Chart

IV. SCHEDULE

- Refer to the Standards (19.0) section of the Software Life Cycle Chart

SOFTWARE DOCUMENTATION CHECKLIST

I. Prepare systems development documentation, which includes:
- ☐ Feasibility Study Document
- ☐ Cost–Benefit Analysis Document
- ☐ Statement of Work
- ☐ Requirements Definition Document, including:
  - ☐ Relational tables
  - ☐ Data-Flow Diagrams, like:
    - ☐ Warnier–Orr
    - ☐ Ward–Mellor
    - ☐ Hatley–Pirbhai
    - ☐ De Marco
    - ☐ Gane and Sarson
  - ☐ Entity relationship diagrams
  - ☐ Process activation tables
  - ☐ Minispecs
  - ☐ Decision Table
  - ☐ Decision Tree
  - ☐ File Description Form
  - ☐ Report Layout Form
  - ☐ Structured English
  - ☐ Data Dictionary listing
- ☐ Alternatives Analysis Document
  - ☐ Data-Flow Diagrams, like:
    - ☐ Warnier–Orr
    - ☐ Ward–Mellor
    - ☐ Hatley–Pirbhai
    - ☐ De Marco
    - ☐ Gane and Sarson
  - ☐ Entity relationship diagrams
  - ☐ Process activation tables
  - ☐ Minispecs
  - ☐ Decision Table
  - ☐ Decision Tree
  - ☐ File Description Form
  - ☐ Report Layout Form
  - ☐ Structured English
  - ☐ Data Dictionary listing

- ☐ Functional Specifications Document, including:
  - ☐ Data-Flow Diagrams, like:
    - ☐ Warnier–Orr
    - ☐ Ward–Mellor
    - ☐ Hatley–Pirbhai
    - ☐ De Marco
    - ☐ Gane and Sarson
  - ☐ Entity relationship diagram
  - ☐ Process activation tables
  - ☐ Minispecs
  - ☐ Decision Tables
  - ☐ File Description Form
  - ☐ Report Layout Form
  - ☐ Structured English
  - ☐ Data Dictionary
- ☐ Preliminary Design Document, including:
  - ☐ Systems Flowchart
  - ☐ Structure Chart
  - ☐ Record Layout Form
  - ☐ File Description Form
  - ☐ Data Models
  - ☐ Structured English
  - ☐ Data Dictionary
- ☐ Detail Design Document, including:
  - ☐ Program Flowchart
  - ☐ Decision Table
  - ☐ Decision Tree
  - ☐ Nassi–Shneiderman Charts
  - ☐ Input–Process–Output Charts
  - ☐ File Description Form
  - ☐ Record Layout Form
  - ☐ Data Dictionary
  - ☐ Unit test plan
- ☐ Verification/Validation document, including:
  - ☐ Verification/Validation Plan
  - ☐ Verification/validation procedures
  - ☐ Verification/validation test reports
- ☐ Integration test document, including:
  - ☐ Subsystem Test Report Form
  - ☐ System Test Report Form
- ☐ Conversion Plan, including:

☐ System Conversion Plan
☐ Data Conversion Plan
☐ Installation and Implementation Document, including:
    ☐ Installation and Implementation Plan
    ☐ Installation and Implementation Package Form
    ☐ Installation and Implementation Test Checklist

II. Prepare sustaining documentation, which includes:
☐ Maintenance, like:
    ☐ Programming Checklist
    ☐ Facility Usage Checklist
    ☐ Equipment Maintenance Report
☐ Enhancements, like:
    ☐ System Upgrade Checklist
    ☐ System Performance Graphs
    ☐ System Productivity Graphs

III. Prepare operations documentation, which includes:
☐ Data Center, like:
    ☐ System Utilization Log Form
    ☐ Machine-run Log Form
    ☐ System Incidence Log Form
    ☐ Software Program Requirement Log Form
    ☐ Software Program Distribution Form
☐ Security, like:
    ☐ Security Plan
    ☐ Computing Facility Controls Checklist
    ☐ System Access Checklist
    ☐ Data Checklists
☐ Documentation, like:
    ☐ User Manual
    ☐ Desk Procedures
    ☐ Computer Operator Manual
☐ Training, like:
    ☐ Training Plan
    ☐ Instructor Guide
    ☐ Student Handout
    ☐ Training Schedule

IV. Prepare administrative documentation, which includes:
☐ Configuration management, like:

- ☐ Configuration Management Plan
- ☐ Software Version Form
- ☐ Problem Report Form and Flowchart
- ☐ Configuration Audit Checklist
- ☐ Patch Request Form
☐ Quality, like:
  - ☐ Software Quality-Assurance Plan
  - ☐ Quality-Circles Checklist
  - ☐ Statistical Quality-Control Graphs
  - ☐ Statistical Quality-Control Checklist
☐ Standards, like:
  - ☐ Standards and Guidelines Manual
  - ☐ Disaster Recovery Plan
  - ☐ Risk Assessment Checklist
  - ☐ Software Documentation Checklist
☐ Project management, like:
  - ☐ Bar (Gantt) Chart
  - ☐ Activity Relationship Report Form
  - ☐ Network Diagram
  - ☐ Work Breakdown Structure
  - ☐ Resource Histogram
  - ☐ Organization Charts
  - ☐ Status Update Form
  - ☐ Resource Usage Report Form
  - ☐ Project Schedule Report Form
  - ☐ Monthly Status Report Form
  - ☐ Project Cost Report Form
  - ☐ "S" Cost Curve
☐ Data Center, like:
  - ☐ Manual-Checkout Form
  - ☐ Runbook Checklist
  - ☐ Tape-Reel Archive Form
  - ☐ Scratch-Tape Reuse Form
☐ Subcontractor management, like:
  - ☐ Request for Proposal Plan
  - ☐ Subcontractor Requirements List Form
  - ☐ Performance Validation Checklist

Chapter 20

Project/Program Management

PROJECT PLAN OVERVIEW

I. DESCRIPTION

- A group of documents detailing how a project or program will be planned, organized, and controlled, regarding topics like scheduling, quality assurance, configuration management, and so on

II. OBJECTIVES

- Enable the project manager to more efficiently manage a project
- Handle unforeseen circumstances more effectively
- Coordinate activities better

III. ORGANIZATION

- Refer to MIS Director (1.0), Configuration Management Specialists (1.2.4), Project Manager (1.6), and Steering Committee (2.0) in the Organization and Responsibilities Chart

IV. SCHEDULE

- Refer to the Project/Program Management (20.0) section of the Software Life Cycle Chart

PROJECT PLAN

I. Present title page, which includes:
   A. Document title
   B. Document number
   C. Original release date
   D. Current release date
   E. Current revision number
   F. Appropriate signatures and date

II. Present modifications sheet, which includes:
   A. Sequentially numbered list of changes
   B. Explanation of changes
   C. Page numbers of changes
   D. Appropriate signatures and date

III. Present table of contents, which includes:
   A. Section headings
   B. Chapter titles
   C. Chapter subtitles
   D. Relevant page numbers

IV. Present executive summary, which includes:
   A. Overview
   B. Principal points

V. Present introduction, which includes:
   A. Goals
   B. Scope
   C. Objectives, like:
      • Technical
      • Business
   D. Background information

VI. Describe management plans, which include:
   A. Organization
   B. Schedule

C. Resources
D. Visibility
E. Tracking/monitoring
F. Reporting
G. Training
H. Risk assessment
I. Tasks
J. Budget
K. Reviews
L. Change control
M. Customer liaison
N. Facilities

VII. Describe quality-assurance plan

VIII. Describe configuration management plan, which includes:
A. Accounting
B. Reporting
C. Identification
D. Control

IX. Describe technical plans, which include:
A. System overview, like:
- Inputs
- Processes and functions
- Outputs
- Interfaces
- Constraints and limitations
- Performance criteria

B. Reviews

C. Documentation

D. Standards

E. Methodology

F. Software development life cycle, like:
  - Goals
  - Activities
  - Deliverables

X. Prepare glossary

XI. Attach appendixes

BAR (GANTT) CHART OVERVIEW

I. DESCRIPTION

- Shows the flow time of tasks (that are usually comprised of subtasks reflected in a Network Diagram) and the start and finish dates for each one

II. OBJECTIVE

- Gives an overview of the schedule of a project

III. ORGANIZATION

- Refer to Configuration Management Specialists (1.2.4), Program Planners (1.2.6), and Project Manager (1.6) in the Organization and Responsibilities Chart

IV. SCHEDULE

- Refer to the Project/Program Management (20.0) section of the Software Life Cycle Chart

BAR (GANTT) CHART CHECKLIST

Identify the contents of the bar chart, including:
- ☐ Tasks
- ☐ Durations
- ☐ Task descriptions
- ☐ Timeline, like:
    - ☐ Weekly
    - ☐ Monthly
    - ☐ Quarterly
    - ☐ Semiannually
    - ☐ Annually
- ☐ Task responsibility

BAR (GANTT) CHART

WBS CODE	TASK	PERSON	CRITICAL Y/N?	199X													
				JUNE				JULY				AUGUST			
				WEEK 1	WEEK 2	WEEK 3	WEEK 4	WEEK 1	WEEK 2	WEEK 3	WEEK 4	WEEK 1	WEEK 2	WEEK 3	WEEK 4
3.1.1	BUILD HIPO CHARTS	SMITH	Y												
3.1.2	WRITE PSEUDOCODE	JONES	Y												
3.1.3	VERIFY PSEUDOCODE	KIMS	Y												
3.1.4	BUILD FLOWCHARTS	SMITH	Y												
3.1.5	IDENTIFY OUTPUT	JAMES	N												
3.1.6	IDENTIFY INPUT	COOK	N												

ACTIVITY RELATIONSHIP REPORT FORM OVERVIEW

I. DESCRIPTION

- Shows the dependencies among activities and their relationships

II. OBJECTIVES

- Help identify the logical connections of activities
- Provide effective coordination of those activities

III. ORGANIZATION

- Refer to Program Planners (1.2.6) and Project Manager (1.6) in the Organization and Responsibilities Chart

IV. SCHEDULE

- Refer to the Project/Program Management (20.0) section of the Software Life Cycle Chart

ACTIVITY RELATIONSHIP REPORT FORM

PROJECT: Payroll System

DATE: 8/21/9X

PREDECESSOR	SUCCESSOR	RELATIONSHIP TYPE	LAG	TOTAL FLOAT
1801	1802	START-TO-FINISH	3	17
1802	1803	FINISH-TO-START	2	4
1803	1804	FINISH-TO-START	5	10

ACTIVITY RELATIONSHIP REPORT FORM

PROJECT: Payroll System

DATE:

PREDECESSOR	SUCCESSOR	RELATIONSHIP TYPE	LAG	TOTAL FLOAT

NETWORK DIAGRAMS OVERVIEW

I. DESCRIPTION

- Diagrams showing the sequence of tasks that occur on a project and the respective start and stop times for the project

II. OBJECTIVES

- Provide the project manager with a "road map" to manage the project
- Eliminate repetition of activities
- Keep the project from starting late
- Prevent wasting valuable time

III. ORGANIZATION

- Refer to Configuration Management Specialists (1.2.4), Program Planners (1.2.6), and Project Manager (1.6) in the Organization and Responsibilities Chart

IV. SCHEDULE

- Refer to the Project/Program Management (20.0) section of the Software Life Cycle Chart

NETWORK DIAGRAM CHECKLIST

I. Identify the type of network diagram to develop, such as:
- ☐ Arrow diagram
- ☐ Precedence diagram

II. Determine the contents of the network diagram, including:
- ☐ Tasks
- ☐ Task descriptions
- ☐ Early start dates
- ☐ Early finish dates
- ☐ Late start dates
- ☐ Late finish dates
- ☐ Floats
- ☐ Durations
- ☐ Task sequences

ARROW DIAGRAM

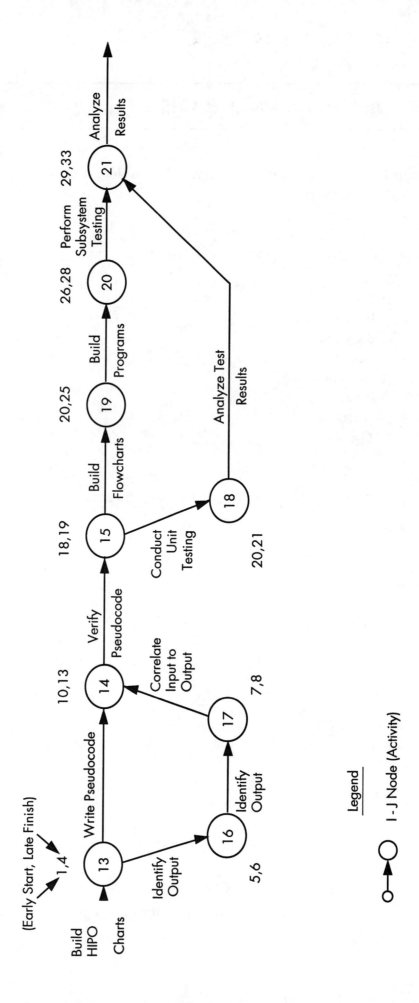

Build HIPO
Charts

(Early Start, Late Finish)
1,4

Write Pseudocode

Identify
Output

Identify
Output

Correlate
Input to
Output

Verify
Pseudocode

Conduct
Unit
Testing

Analyze Test
Results

Build
Flowcharts

Build
Programs

Perform
Subsystem
Testing

Analyze
Results

13

16

17

14

15

18

19

20

21

5,6

7,8

10,13

18,19

20,21

20,25

26,28

29,33

Legend

I - J Node (Activity)

PRECEDENCE DIAGRAM

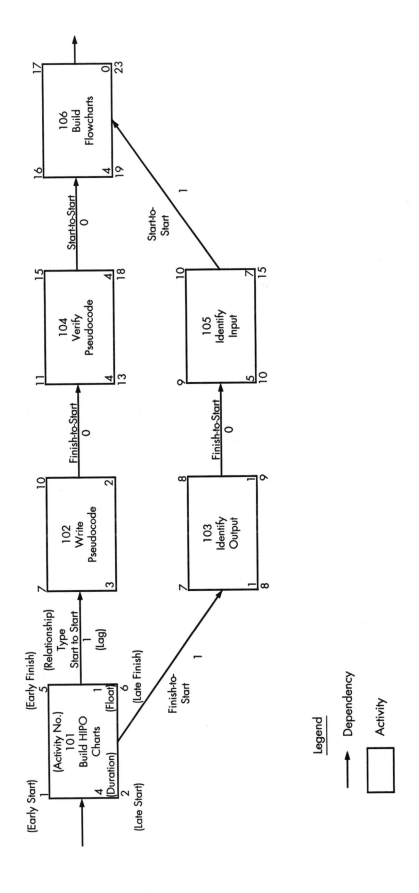

Legend

→ Dependency

☐ Activity

WORK BREAKDOWN STRUCTURE OVERVIEW

I. DESCRIPTION

- Shows hierarchically the tasks and subtasks in an inverted tree format that will be performed on a project

II. OBJECTIVES

- Improve communication by identifying specifically what tasks to perform
- Serve as the basis for accurate and reliable time estimates and schedules
- Build accountability once responsibilities are assigned to each task and subtask
- Enable more effective decisions regarding staff hiring and retention

III. ORGANIZATION

- Refer to Configuration Management Specialists (1.2.4), Program Planners (1.2.6), and Project Manager (1.6) in the Organization and Responsibilities Chart

IV. SCHEDULE

- Refer to the Project/Program Management (20.0) section of the Software Life Cycle Chart

WORK BREAKDOWN STRUCTURE
(BY TASK ONLY)

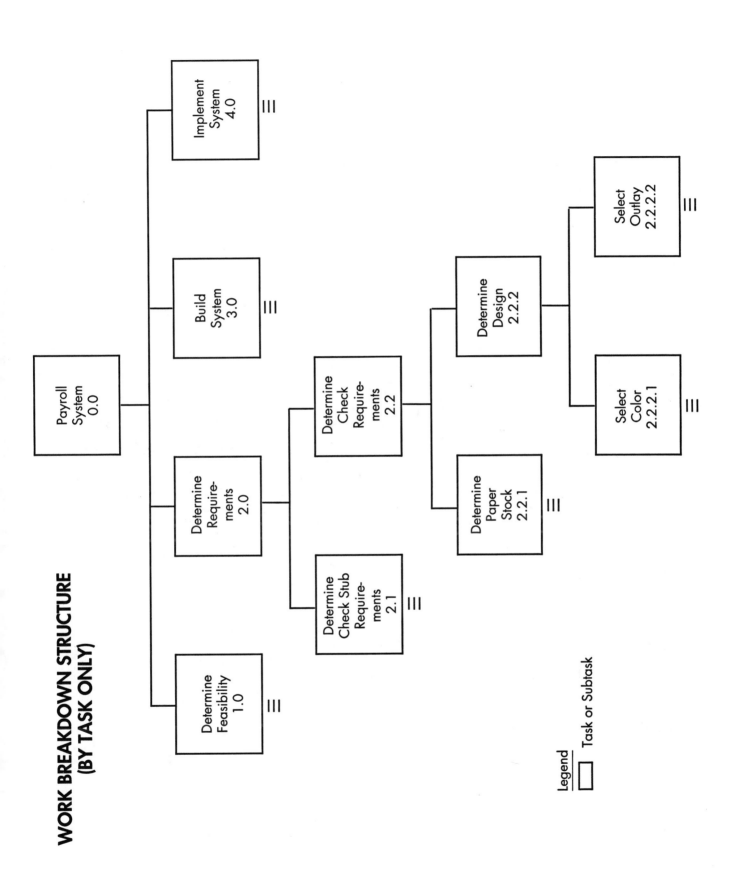

Legend

☐ Task or Subtask

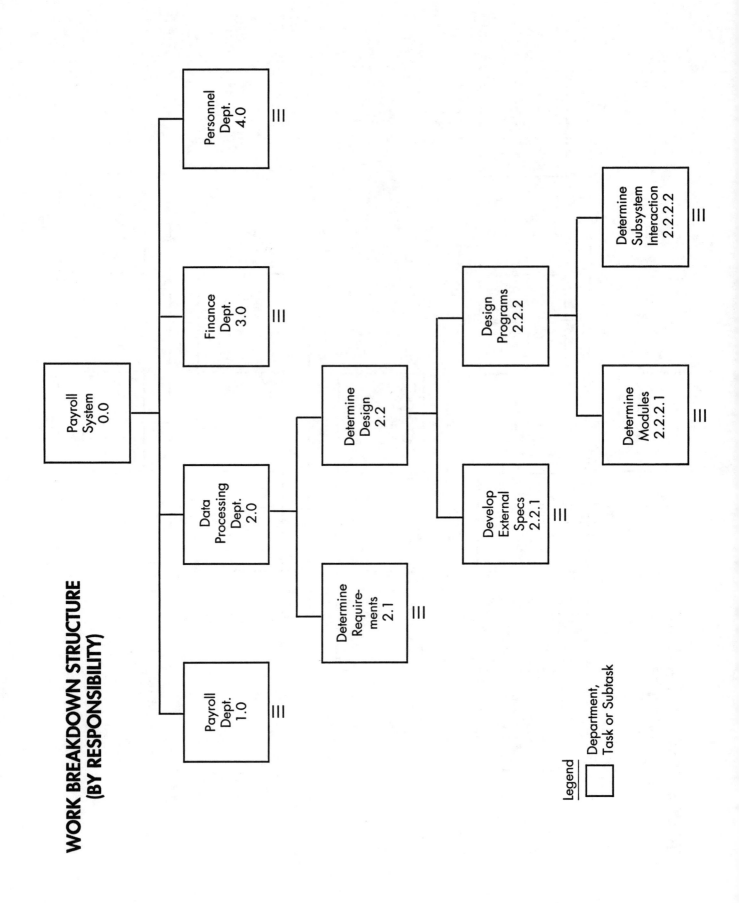

**WORK BREAKDOWN STRUCTURE
(BY RESPONSIBILITY)**

Payroll System 0.0

Payroll Dept. 1.0

Data Processing Dept. 2.0

Finance Dept. 3.0

Personnel Dept. 4.0

Determine Requirements 2.1

Determine Design 2.2

Develop External Specs 2.2.1

Design Programs 2.2.2

Determine Modules 2.2.2.1

Determine Subsystem Interaction 2.2.2.2

Legend

Department, Task or Subtask

WORK BREAKDOWN STRUCTURE (BY PRODUCT)

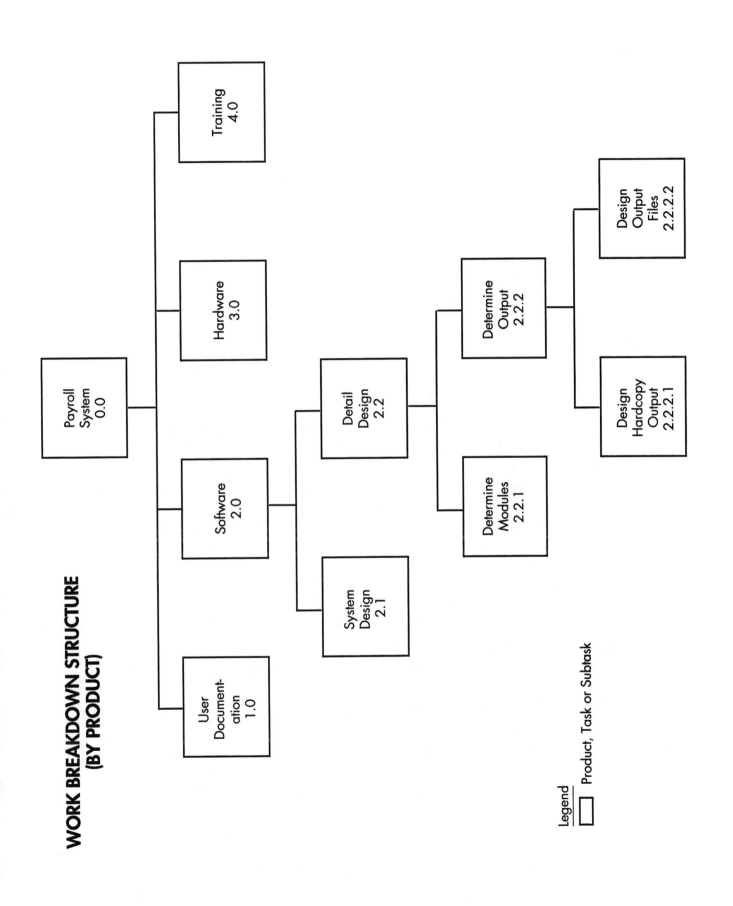

Payroll System 0.0

- User Document-ation 1.0
- Software 2.0
- Hardware 3.0
- Training 4.0

Software 2.0
- System Design 2.1
- Detail Design 2.2

Detail Design 2.2
- Determine Modules 2.2.1
- Determine Output 2.2.2

Determine Output 2.2.2
- Design Hardcopy Output 2.2.2.1
- Design Output Files 2.2.2.2

Legend

☐ Product, Task or Subtask

RESOURCE HISTOGRAM OVERVIEW

I. DESCRIPTION

- Shows a profile of how one or more people are, or will be, used on a project over a period of time

II. OBJECTIVES

- Look at cost-effectiveness for employing one or more individuals on a project
- Identify spots where too much overtime, for example, is occurring and where individuals will remain idle
- Readjust resource assignments to "level," or smooth, the histogram to reflect better management of resources

III. ORGANIZATION

- Refer to Program Planners (1.2.6) and Project Manager (1.6) in the Organization and Responsibilities Chart

IV. SCHEDULE

- Refer to the Project/Program Management (20.0) section of the Software Life Cycle Chart

RESOURCE HISTOGRAM (UNLEVELED)

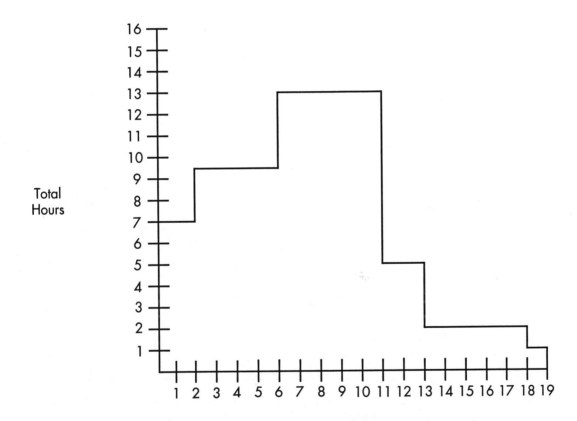

Total
Hours

Time Frame
(Days, Weeks, or Months)

RESOURCE HISTOGRAM (LEVELED)

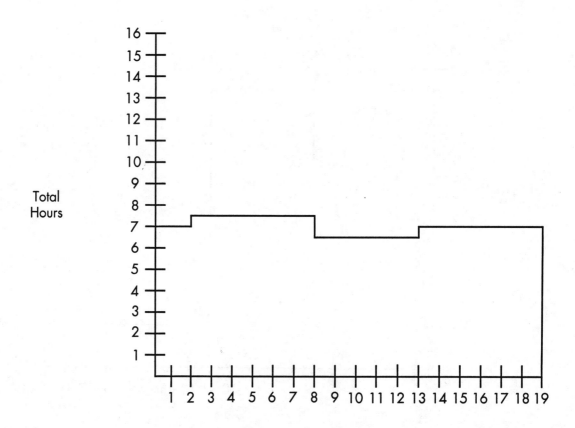

Time Frame
(Days, Weeks, or Months)

ORGANIZATION CHARTS OVERVIEW

I. DESCRIPTION

- Reflects the relationships among participants in a data processing organization

II. OBJECTIVES

- Identify reporting relationships
- Improve communication
- Build accountability
- Improve coordination

III. ORGANIZATION

- Refer to MIS Director (1.0), Manager of Development (1.1), Supervisor of Analysis (1.1.1, 1.4.1), Supervisor of Design (1.1.2), Supervisor of Programming (1.1.3, 1.4.2), Manager of Technical Support (1.2), Manager of Operations (1.3), Supervisor of Computer Operations (1.3.1), Supervisor of Control and Scheduling (1.3.2), Supervisor of Data Entry (1.3.3), Supervisor of Production (1.3.4), Manager of Sustaining (1.4), Manager of Subcontract Support (1.5), and Project Manager (1.6) in the Organization and Responsibilities Chart

IV. SCHEDULE

- Refer to Project/Program Managemt nt (20.0) section of the Software Life Cycle Chart

SUSTAINING ORGANIZATIONAL STRUCTURE (MAINTENANCE)

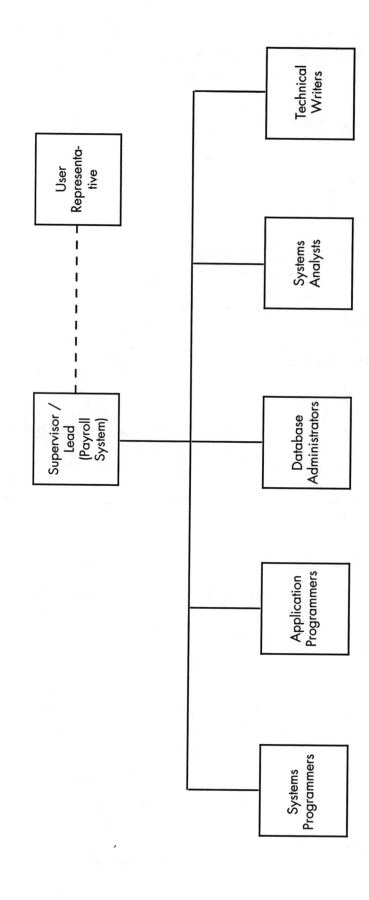

TASK FORCE ORGANIZATIONAL STRUCTURE
(DEVELOPMENT)

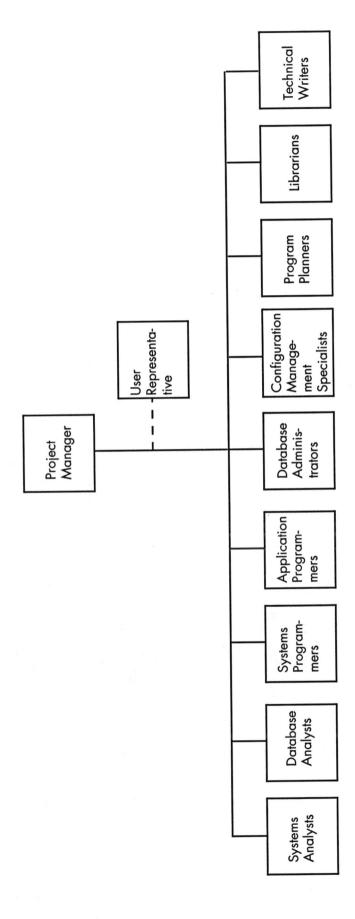

MATRIX ORGANIZATIONAL STRUCTURE
(DEVELOPMENT)

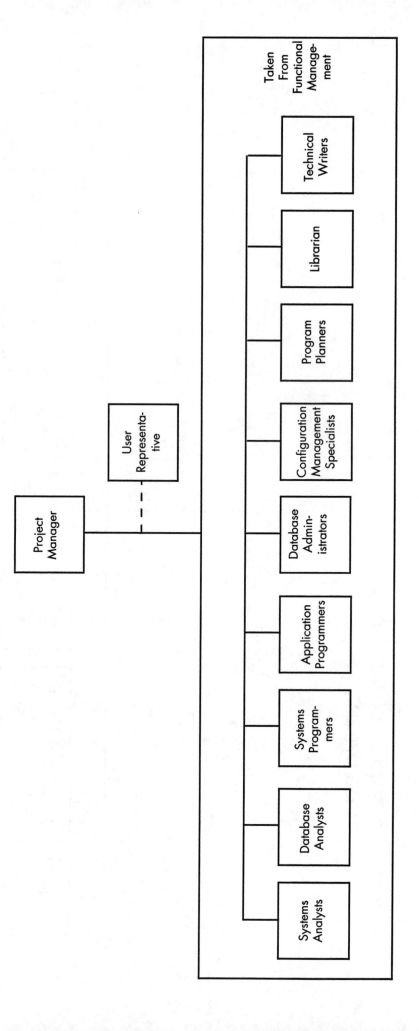

STATUS UPDATE FORM OVERVIEW

I. DESCRIPTION

- Records status, or amount of completion of each task in a Network Diagram or Bar Chart

II. OBJECTIVES

- Document the amount of completion per task
- Provide an audit trail to trace the accuracy of that completion
- Enable tracking and monitoring of progress regarding those activities

III. ORGANIZATION

- Refer to Program Planners (1.2.6) and Project Manager (1.6) in the Organization and Responsibilities Chart

IV. SCHEDULE

- Refer to the Project/Program Management (20.0) section of the Software Life Cycle Chart

STATUS UPDATE FORM

PROJECT: Payroll System

DATE: 4/3/9X

ACTIVITY NO.	ACTIVITY DESCRIPTION	DURATION	ESTIMATED REMAINING DURATION	ESTIMATED PERCENT COMPLETE	ACTUAL START	ACTUAL FINISH
1505	Build Module X455.1	5 days	3 days	40	3/17/9X	
1510	Build Module X460.1	10 days	0	100	3/21/9X	3/31/9X
1515	Build Module X465.1	6 days	3	50	3/22/9x	

STATUS UPDATE FORM

PROJECT: Payroll System

DATE: 4/3/9X

ACTIVITY NO.	ACTIVITY DESCRIPTION	DURATION	ESTIMATED REMAINING DURATION	ESTIMATED PERCENT COMPLETE	ACTUAL START	ACTUAL FINISH

RESOURCE USAGE REPORT FORM OVERVIEW

I. DESCRIPTION

- Shows data on the planned, actual, and projected uses of resources assigned to a project

II. OBJECTIVES

- Help the project manager track and monitor utilization of resources
- Determine how to more cost-effectively employ resources
- Respond more efficiently to circumstances requiring corrective action

III. ORGANIZATION

- Refer to Program Planners (1.2.6) and Project Manager (1.6) in the Organization and Responsibilities Chart

IV. SCHEDULE

- Refer to the Project/Program Management (20.0) section of the Software Life Cycle Chart

RESOURCE USAGE REPORT FORM

PROJECT: Payroll System

DATE: 3/23/9X

ACTIVITY NO.	RESOURCE DESCRIPTION	RESOURCE TYPE	UNIT	UNIT PRICE	QUANTITY	COST TO DATE
1304	Smith, Joe	Labor	1	$35/hr	1	$1,300
1304	Franks, Mary	Labor	1	$32.50/hr	1	$1,100
1305	Microcomputer	Computer	1	$3,500 ea.	2	$7,000

RESOURCE USAGE REPORT FORM

PROJECT: Payroll System

DATE: 3/23/9X

ACTIVITY NO.	RESOURCE DESCRIPTION	RESOURCE TYPE	UNIT	UNIT PRICE	QUANTITY	COST TO DATE

RESOURCE USAGE FORM OVERVIEW

I. DESCRIPTION

- Records data on the usage of a resource employed on one or more activities

II. OBJECTIVES

- Document the resource type and amount used on an activity basis
- Provide an audit trail to trace how resources have been used
- Enable tracking and monitoring of costs regarding a resource or resources

III. ORGANIZATION

- Refer to Program Planners (1.2.6) and Project Manager (1.6) in the Organization and Responsibilities Chart

IV. SCHEDULE

- Refer to the Project/Program Management (20.0) section of the Software Life Cycle Chart

RESOURCE USAGE FORM

PROJECT: Payroll System

DATE: 3/17/9X

RESOURCE DESCRIPTION	RESOURCE TYPE	ACTIVITY NO.	ACTIVITY DESCRIPTION	UNIT	UNIT PRICE	QUANTITY
Smith, Joe	Labor	1705	Build structure chart	1	$27/hr	1
Brown, Cindy	Labor	1710	Draft entity relationship diagrams	1	$31/hr	1
Microcomputer	Computer	1715	Draft data-flow diagrams	1	$3,500 ea	1

RESOURCE USAGE FORM

PROJECT:

DATE:

RESOURCE DESCRIPTION	RESOURCE TYPE	ACTIVITY NO.	ACTIVITY DESCRIPTION	UNIT	UNIT PRICE	QUANTITY

PROJECT SCHEDULE REPORT FORM OVERVIEW

I. DESCRIPTION

- Displays the time each activity is projected to start or stop or has actually started or stopped, its float, its narrative description, its variance, and its activity number

II. OBJECTIVES

- Help the project manager know the schedule status of each activity and the entire project
- Improve communication and coordination by informing staff members of the degree to which tasks have been completed

III. ORGANIZATION

- Refer to Configuration Management Specialists (1.2.4), Program Planners (1.2.6), and Project Manager (1.6) in the Organization and Responsibilities Chart

IV. SCHEDULE

- Refer to the Project/Program Management (20.0) section of the Software Life Cycle Chart

PROJECT SCHEDULE REPORT FORM

PROJECT: Payroll System

ACTIVITY NO.	ACTIVITY DESCRIPTION	ESTIMATED DURATION	REMAINING DURATION	EARLY START	EARLY FINISH	LATE START	LATE FINISH	ACTUAL START	ACTUAL FINISH	FLOAT
1005	Build Module X345.1	10 days	9 days	3/21	3/30	3/22	3/31	3/21		1
1010	Build Module X350.1	5 days	0 day	3/21	3/25	3/21	3/25	3/21	3/25	0
1015	Build Module X355.1	3 days	1 day	3/22	3/24	3/23	3/25	3/22		1

PROJECT SCHEDULE REPORT FORM

PROJECT: DATE:

ACTIVITY NO.	ACTIVITY DESCRIPTION	ESTIMATED DURATION	REMAINING DURATION	EARLY START	EARLY FINISH	LATE START	LATE FINISH	ACTUAL START	ACTUAL FINISH	FLOAT

MONTHLY STATUS REPORT FORM OVERVIEW

I. DESCRIPTION

- Provides overall assessment on the status of a project regarding cost, schedule, and quality

II. OBJECTIVES

- Help the project manager track and monitor how well the project is progressing
- Determine if work-arounds are necessary
- Respond more efficiently and effectively to circumstances requiring corrective action

III. ORGANIZATION

- Refer to Program Planners (1.2.6), Project Manager (1.6), and Steering Committee (2.0) in the Organization and Responsibilities Chart

IV. SCHEDULE

- Refer to the Project/Program Management (20.0) section of the Software Life Cycle Chart

MONTHLY STATUS REPORT FORM

PROJECT: Payroll System

DATE: 7/21/9X

SCHEDULE

(BASELINE) START: 1/17/8X

(BASELINE) FINISH: 9/3/9X

ACTUAL START: 1/17/8X

ESTIMATED COMPLETION DATE: 10/23/9X

VARIANCE: 224 days

BUDGET

ORIGINAL TOTAL COST ESTIMATE: $1.3 billion

ESTIMATED COST TO DATE: $1.7 million

ACTUAL COST TO DATE: $1.9 million

ESTIMATED COST AT COMPLETION: $2.3 million

VARIANCE: $400,000

OVERALL PERFORMANCE EVALUATION

The project currently is behind schedule and exceeds estimates. This circumstance is the result of unanticipated complexity in building code as well as poor specifications prepared earlier. Also, severe turnover of personnel has occurred, which has delayed progress.

MONTHLY STATUS REPORT FORM

PROJECT: DATE:

SCHEDULE

(BASELINE) START:

(BASELINE) FINISH:

ACTUAL START:

ESTIMATED COMPLETION DATE:

VARIANCE:

BUDGET

ORIGINAL TOTAL COST ESTIMATE:

ESTIMATED COST TO DATE:

ACTUAL COST TO DATE:

ESTIMATED COST AT COMPLETION:

VARIANCE:

OVERALL PERFORMANCE EVALUATION

PROJECT COST REPORT FORM OVERVIEW

I. DESCRIPTION

- Displays the time each activity is projected to start and finish or has actually started or finished, its narrative description, the activity number, the budgeted cost, the actual cost, the estimated cost to complete, and variances (the differences between planned and actual at a given point in time)

II. OBJECTIVES

- Help the project manager know the cost status of each activity and the entire project
- Maintain financial control over it
- Change resources and strategies based on plans

III. ORGANIZATION

- Refer to Program Planners (1.2.6) and Project Manager (1.6) in the Organization and Responsibilities Chart

IV. SCHEDULE

- Refer to the Project/Program Management (20.0) section of the Software Life Cycle Chart

PROJECT COST REPORT FORM

PROJECT: Payroll System

DATE: 3/26/9X

ACTIVITY NO.	ACTIVITY DESCRIPTION	EARLY START	EARLY FINISH	FLOAT	ORIGINAL ESTIMATE TO DATE	ACTUAL TO DATE	ORIGINAL TOTAL ESTIMATE	ESTIMATE TO COMPLETE	VARIANCE
1301	Build FICA module	1/13	2/24	5	$3,000	$3,200	$5,000	$5,500	$500
1302	Build state tax module	1/15	2/23	2	$2,100	$2,100	$3,000	$3,000	$0
1303	Build federal tax module	1/15	2/23	2	$5,700	$5,900	$6,000	$6,200	$200

PROJECT COST REPORT FORM

PROJECT: DATE:

ACTIVITY NO.	ACTIVITY DESCRIPTION	EARLY START	EARLY FINISH	FLOAT	ORIGINAL ESTIMATE TO DATE	ACTUAL TO DATE	ORIGINAL TOTAL ESTIMATE	ESTIMATE TO COMPLETE	VARIANCE

"S" COST CURVE OVERVIEW

I. DESCRIPTION

- A cumulative curve displaying the accumulation of costs over a period of time

II. OBJECTIVES

- Help the project manager track and monitor costs
- Determine trends regarding project costs
- Determine if circumstances require corrective action

III. ORGANIZATION

- Refer to Program Planners (1.2.6) and Project Manager (1.6) in the Organization and Responsibilities Chart

IV. SCHEDULE

- Refer to the Project/Program Management (20.0) section of the Software Life Cycle Chart

"S" COST CURVE

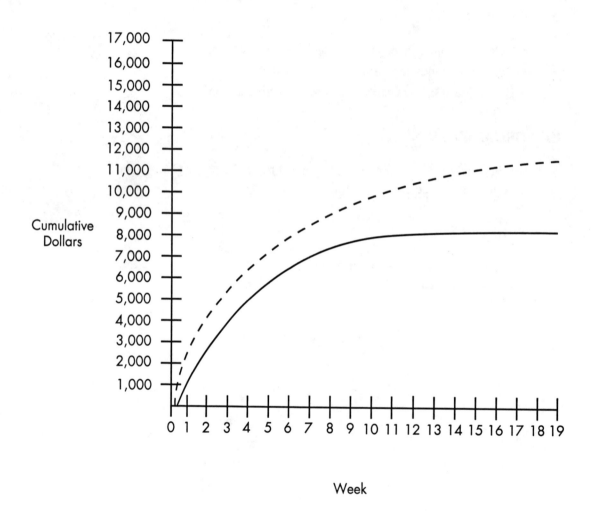

Cumulative Dollars

17,000
16,000
15,000
14,000
13,000
12,000
11,000
10,000
9,000
8,000
7,000
6,000
5,000
4,000
3,000
2,000
1,000

0 1 2 3 4 5 6 7 8 9 10 11 12 13 14 15 16 17 18 19

Week

Legend

– – – Planned
——— Actual

DIRECTIVES CHECKLIST OVERVIEW

I. DESCRIPTION

- Identifies all the topics that project procedures should address

II. OBJECTIVES

- Help avoid overlooking a critical topic
- Improve communication by identifying potential areas of ambiguity
- Help to conduct cost-effective administration of projects

III. ORGANIZATION

- Refer to Program Planner (1.2.6) and Project Manager (1.6) in the Organization and Responsibilities Chart

IV. SCHEDULE

- Refer to the Project/Program Management (20.0) section of the Software Life Cycle Chart

DIRECTIVES OUTLINE

I. Identify purpose

II. Identify scope

III. Identify objectives

IV. List references

V. Describe tasks and responsibilities

VI. Add exhibits

VII. Prepare glossary

VIII. Attach appendixes

DIRECTIVES CHECKLIST

I. Project management, which includes:
- ☐ Prepare planning directives that address:
  - ☐ Estimating
  - ☐ Scheduling
  - ☐ Visibility
  - ☐ Risk assessment
  - ☐ Work breakdown structure
  - ☐ Budgeting
- ☐ Prepare organizing directives that address:
  - ☐ Resource allocation, like:
    - ☐ People
    - ☐ Equipment
    - ☐ Software
    - ☐ Facilities
  - ☐ Resource selection, like:
    - ☐ People
    - ☐ Equipment
    - ☐ Software
    - ☐ Facilities
  - ☐ Training
  - ☐ Meetings
  - ☐ Project communication
- ☐ Prepare controlling directives that address:
  - ☐ Status collection
  - ☐ Reports
  - ☐ Corrective action and contingency planning
  - ☐ Status assessment
  - ☐ Change control
  - ☐ Project history
  - ☐ Schedule performance monitoring
  - ☐ Budget performance monitoring
  - ☐ Reviews

II. Technical operations, which include:
- ☐ Prepare configuration management directives that address:
  - ☐ Identification
  - ☐ Accounting

- [ ] Reporting
- [ ] Control
- [ ] Prepare quality-assurance directives that address:
  - [ ] Company standards
  - [ ] Industry standards
  - [ ] Reliability
  - [ ] Testability
  - [ ] Measurability
- [ ] Prepare life-cycle directives that address:
  - [ ] Feasibility Study Document
  - [ ] Requirements Definition Document
  - [ ] Alternatives Analysis Document
  - [ ] Preliminary Design Document
  - [ ] Detail Design Document
  - [ ] Test Plan
  - [ ] Installation and Implementation Plan
- [ ] Prepare systems and audit directives
- [ ] Prepare life cycle approach directives
- [ ] Prepare system overview directives
- [ ] Prepare methodology directives

Chapter 21

Data Center—
Administrative

MANUAL-CHECKOUT FORM OVERVIEW

I. DESCRIPTION

- Provides formal method of checking out reference manuals

II. OBJECTIVES

- Determine, maintain control over, and provide audit trail for who has a copy of which document

III. ORGANIZATION

- Refer to Configuration Management Specialists (1.2.4) and Distribution Clerks (1.3.4.1) in the Organization and Responsibilities Chart

IV. SCHEDULE

- Refer to the Feasibility (1.0), Requirements (2.0), Alternatives (3.0), Specifications (4.0), Design (5.0), Code and Test (6.0), Verification/ Validation (7.0), Integration (8.0), Conversion (9.0), Installation and Integration (10.0), Maintenance (11.0), and Enhancements (12.0) phases and the Data Center—Administrative (21.0) section of the Software Life Cycle Chart

MANUAL CHECKOUT FORM

MANUAL NAME Software Specifications	MANUAL # SP123XX	REVISION # C	MANUAL DESCRIPTION Functional Specifications		

REQUESTOR'S NAME J. Paulson	REQUESTOR'S PHONE # x-21xx	REQUESTOR'S ADDRESS Building 2X	DATE OUT 05/10/XX	DATE IN 06/10/XX	DATE DUE 06/15/XX

MANUAL CHECKOUT FORM

MANUAL NAME _____

MANUAL # _____

REVISION # _____

MANUAL DESCRIPTION _____

REQUESTOR'S
NAME _____

REQUESTOR'S
PHONE # _____

REQUESTOR'S
ADDRESS _____

DATE
OUT _____

DATE
IN _____

DATE
DUE _____

RUNBOOK CHECKLIST OVERVIEW

I. DESCRIPTION

- Identifies a job, its corresponding steps and their sequences, its files, and its programs
- One runbook exists for each job

II. OBJECTIVES

- Document major activities of a job
- Improve communication and understanding among computing professionals
- Provide basis for configuration management and change control

III. ORGANIZATION

- Refer to Systems Programmers (1.1.3.1, 1.3.2.2, 1.4.2.1), Application Programmers (1.1.3.2, 1.4.2.2), Systems Librarians (1.2.1), and Job Schedulers (1.3.2.1) in the Organization and Responsibilities Chart

IV. SCHEDULE

- Refer to the Data Center—Administrative (21.0) section of the Software Life Cycle Chart

RUNBOOK CHECKLIST

- [ ] Prepare title page, including:
  - [ ] Job identification
  - [ ] Job description
- [ ] Prepare any special instructions, including:
  - [ ] Restart considerations
- [ ] Prepare system flowchart, including:
  - [ ] Input data
  - [ ] Job steps
  - [ ] Output data
- [ ] Prepare message page, including:
  - [ ] Messages
  - [ ] Explanations
  - [ ] Actions
- [ ] Prepare approval checklist
- [ ] Record job scheduling considerations, including:
  - [ ] Run schedules
  - [ ] Priorities
- [ ] Prepare runbook revision log, including:
  - [ ] Revision date
  - [ ] Work-order number
  - [ ] Purpose of revisions
- [ ] Record job resource requirements, including:
  - [ ] Required resources
  - [ ] Steps
- [ ] Prepare job control language (JCL) deck description sheet, including:
  - [ ] Photocopies
  - [ ] Card descriptions
- [ ] Prepare installation record
- [ ] Design and prepare sample forms, including:
  - [ ] Form names
  - [ ] Form specifications
- [ ] Prepare program/procedure listing
- [ ] Prepare record layouts
- [ ] Prepare file descriptions

TAPE-REEL ARCHIVE FORM OVERVIEW

I. DESCRIPTION

- Provides fast and efficient method of recording storage, retrieval, and archiving of tape reels

II. OBJECTIVE

- Maintain tape-reel audit trail

III. ORGANIZATION

- Refer to Tape/Disk Librarians (1.3.1.1) in the Organization and Responsibilities Chart

IV. SCHEDULE

- Refer to the Code and Test (6.0), Verification/Validation (7.0), Integration (8.0), Conversion (9.0), Installation and Integration (10.0), Maintenance (11.0), and Enhancements (12.0) phases and the Data Center—Administrative (21.0) section of the Software Life Cycle Chart

TAPE-REEL ARCHIVE FORM

FILE IDENTIFICATION	REEL	REEL LENGTH	REEL IDENTIFICATION	DATE IN	COMMENTS
Vacatimu	1 of 1	1XX	123XXX	10-09-XX	

TAPE-REEL ARCHIVE FORM

FILE IDENTIFICATION	REEL	REEL LENGTH	REEL IDENTIFICATION	DATE IN	COMMENTS

SCRATCH-TAPE REUSE FORM OVERVIEW

I. DESCRIPTION

- Provides fast and efficient method of recording storage, retrieval, and distribution of scratch tapes

II. OBJECTIVE

- Maintain scratch-tape reuse audit trail

III. ORGANIZATION

- Refer to Tape/Disk Librarians (1.3.1.1) in the Organization and Responsibilities Chart

IV. SCHEDULE

- Refer to the Code and Test (6.0), Verification/Validation (7.0), Integration (8.0), Conversion (9.0), Installation and Integration (10.0), Maintenance (11.0), and Enhancements (12.0) phases and the Data Center— Administrative (21.0) section of the Software Life Cycle Chart

SCRATCH-TAPE REUSE FORM

WEEK OF: May 5, 19XX

NUMBER OF TAPES AVAILABLE: 1

REEL IDENTIFICATION	REEL LENGTH	ISSUED TO	DATE	SOFTWARE DESCRIPTION
131XX	3XX	R. Goulf	05-07-XX	Travel authorization utility program

SCRATCH-TAPE REUSE FORM

WEEK OF:
NUMBER OF TAPES AVAILABLE:

REEL IDENTIFICATION	REEL LENGTH	ISSUED TO	DATE	SOFTWARE DESCRIPTION

Chapter 22

Subcontract Management

REQUEST FOR PROPOSAL PLAN OVERVIEW

I. DESCRIPTION

- Procures subcontract management products and services
- Provides formal disciplines for the decision-making process

II. OBJECTIVES

- Evaluate and choose subcontractor support
- Set forth procedures, management, control, and evaluation processes

III. ORGANIZATION

- Refer to Manager of Subcontract Support (1.5) and Project Manager (1.6) in the Organization and Responsibilities Chart

IV. SCHEDULE

- Refer to the Requirements (2.0) and Alternatives (3.0) phases and the Subcontract Management (22.0) section of the Software Life Cycle Chart

REQUEST FOR PROPOSAL PLAN

I. Present title page, which includes:
   A. Document title
   B. Document number
   C. Original release date
   D. Current release date
   E. Current revision number
   F. Appropriate signatures and date

II. Present modifications sheet, which includes:
   A. Sequentially numbered list of changes
   B. Explanation of changes
   C. Page numbers of changes
   D. Appropriate signatures and date

III. Present table of contents, which includes:
   A. Section headings
   B. Chapter titles
   C. Chapter subtitles
   D. Relevant page numbers

IV. Present executive summary, which includes:
   A. Overview
   B. Principal features

V. Present introduction, which includes:
   A. Goals
   B. Scope
   C. Objectives, like:
      • Technical
      • Business
   D. Background information

VI. Identify and document management items, which include:
   A. Statement of Work
   B. Proposal response instructions

C. Evaluation criteria
D. Scoring procedures
E. Schedule of deliverables
F. Manpower commitments
G. Audit Plan
H. Project Plan
I. Configuration Management Plan
J. Software Quality-assurance Plan
K. Disaster Recovery Plan
L. Security Plan
M. Data Center—Operations Plan
N. Training Plan
O. User Manual
P. Special considerations

VII. Identify and document technical items, which include:
A. Requirements Definition Document
B. Functional Specifications Document
C. System models
D. Subsystem models
E. Process models
F. Test Plan
G. Verification/Validation Plan
H. System Conversion Plan
I. Data Conversion Plan
J. Installation and Implementation Plan
K. Subcontractor Requirements List Form
L. Special considerations

VIII. Identify and document business items, which include:
    A. Costing instructions
    B. Pricing instructions
    C. Vendor's experience
    D. Vendor's performance history
    E. Contract terms and conditions
    F. Warranties
    G. Make, buy, or lease options
    H. Special considerations

IX. Prepare glossary

X. Attach appendixes

SUBCONTRACTOR REQUIREMENTS LIST FORM OVERVIEW

I. DESCRIPTION

- Guarantee a comprehensive, formal itemized set of end-item deliverables
- Provide a summary of requirements referencing specifications

II. OBJECTIVE

- Identify listing of end item deliverables provided by subcontractor

III. ORGANIZATION

- Refer to Subcontract Support (1.5) and Project Manager (1.6) in the Organization and Responsibilities Chart

IV. SCHEDULE

- Refer to the Requirements (2.0) and Alternatives (3.0) phases and the Subcontract Management (22.0) section of the Software Life Cycle Chart

SUBCONTRACTOR REQUIREMENTS LIST FORM

DOCUMENT REFERENCE
17-AX

REVISION #
1

DOCUMENT REFERENCE DATE
09-09-XX

REQUIREMENT DESCRIPTION
Manage, release, change management, software documentation control, and distribution

END ITEM
Configuration Management Plan

SUBCONTRACTOR REQUIREMENTS LIST FORM

END
ITEM

REQUIREMENT
DESCRIPTION

DOCUMENT
REFERENCE

REVISION
#

DOCUMENT
REFERENCE
DATE

PERFORMANCE VALIDATION CHECKLIST OVERVIEW

I. DESCRIPTION

- Provides list of task performances for subcontractor deliverables

II. OBJECTIVE

- Ensure that tasks meet with acceptance criteria
  — Checked and compared
  — Tested and validated

III. ORGANIZATION

- Refer to Manager of Technical Support (1.2), Configuration Management Specialists (1.2.4), Quality-Assurance Specialists (1.2.5), Testers (1.2.7), and Computing Auditors (1.2.8) in the Organization and Responsibilities Chart

IV. SCHEDULE

- Refer to the Code and Test (6.0), Verification/Validation (7.0), Integration (8.0), Conversion (9.0), Installation and Integration (10.0), Maintenance (11.0), and Enhancements (12.0) phases and Subcontract Management (22.0) section of the Software Life Cycle Chart

PERFORMANCE VALIDATION CHECKLIST

I. Accept and document development deliverables, including:
- ☐ Requirements traceability
- ☐ Specifications adherence
- ☐ Design models structure
- ☐ Code and testing results and performance
- ☐ Integration testing results and performance
- ☐ Installation and implementation testing and performance

II. Accept and document administrative deliverables, including:
- ☐ Subcontractor deliverables exactly match subcontractor requirements list
- ☐ Formal reviews
- ☐ Configuration audits performed and accepted
- ☐ Client response to subcontractor efforts/endeavors monitored
- ☐ Staff training and expenses budgeted

III. Accept and document contractual deliverables, including:
- ☐ Software ownership identified
- ☐ Software upgrade responsibilities established
- ☐ System maintenance responsibilities identified
- ☐ Appropriate warranties identified and understood

GLOSSARY

Activity Relationship Report Form	Shows the dependencies among activities and the type of relationships
Alternatives Analysis Document	Describes the various alternatives that a computing solution can take and provides a recommendation on which alternative to pursue
Audit Plan	Describes audits planned for existing and new computing systems and processing facilities
Bar (Gantt) Chart	Shows the flow time of tasks and the start and finish dates for each one
Computer Operator Manual	Gives instructions on the use and operation of a computer, including hardware and software
Computing Facility Controls Checklist	Details those items that must be secure in a data processing facility, such as a data center or a system library
Configuration Audit Checklist	Ensures the configuration items' test results concur with requirements (known as a functional audit) and that documentation concurs with specifications (known as a physical audit)
Configuration Management Plan	Provides guidelines for managing software documentation and distribution, including release and change activities
Cost–Benefit Analysis Document	An objective cost appraisal of each alternative in the Alternatives Analysis Document
Database Design Flowchart	Displays the logical structure of the database
Database Specifications Document	Establish procedures and processes for database design and support and to provide plans for environments, testing, and backup and recovery
Data Center—Operations Checklist	Establishes data center procedures
Data Center—Operations Plan	Provides test bed for the validation of computing concepts in a real-life environment without having a complete system
Data Conversion Checklist	Provides list of requirements, definitions, standards, and performance for data conversion activity

Data Conversion Plan	Achieves a flexible environment for data conversion
Data Dictionary	Defines data in terms of meaning, format, and usage
Data-Flow Diagrams	Displays the functions and data required for a system to operate
Data Models	Shows the relationships among data in a system and their attributes
Decision Table	Shows the conditions that can occur, the possible combinations thereof, and the action or actions to take in response to those conditions
Decision Tree	Shows the conditions that can occur, the possible combinations thereof, and the action or actions to take in response to those conditions
Desk Procedures	Gives details on conducting administrative actions
Detail Design Document	Describes the exact specifications of the program and data that will be incorporated in the new computing system
Directives Checklist	Lists all the topics that project procedures should address
Disaster Recovery Plan	Details the actions, resources, and priorities to pursue when a disaster, man-made or natural, strikes a data processing department
Equipment Maintenance Report Form	Identifies installation, replacement, and repair activities
Facility Usage Checklist	Provides facilities usage requirements
Feasibility Study Document	Records the analysis conducted to determine whether a computer solution to a problem or circumstance is practical
File Archive Form	Identifies the most current file, associated attributes, and release date
File Description Form	Shows the composition of a file, its format, and its structure
File Request Form	Requests for the most current file and associated attributes
Functional Specifications Document	Describes how the system will appear to the user and the design of the system
Hierarchy–Input–Process– Output Documentation	Illustrates the data and functions performed on that data and the corresponding output of those functions

Installation and Implementation Package Form	Provides information required for each work package to control software package delivery
Installation and Implementation Plan	Identifies provisions necessary to meet with functional requirements and design as defined in specifications and convert those programs
Installation and Implementation Checklist	Addresses operational and administrative installation and implementation
Instructor's Guide	Explains, page-by-page, course material, especially what is incorporated in the student handout
Machine-Run Log Form	Provides machine-run activities, e.g. media used, change activity, and program custodian
Maintenance Control Report Form	Provides current quality assurance status of software
Manual-Checkout Form	Provides formal method of checking out reference manuals
Monthly Status Report Form	Presents an overall assessment on the status of a project regarding cost, schedule, and quality
Nassi–Shneiderman	A visual display of the steps and the logical sequence of those steps to be incorporated in a program
Network Diagrams	Illustrates the sequence of tasks that occur on a project and the respective start and stop times
Organization Charts	Illustrates the relationships among participants in a data processing organization
Patch Request Form	Provides temporary software fixes until a permanent one(s) can be installed
Performance Validation Checklist	Provides list of task performances for subcontractor deliverables
Preliminary Design Document	Describes the logical and physical design of a system that will be constructed during the detail design phase of a project
Problem Report Form and Flowchart	Identifies problems, requests resolution, and documents software and hardware issues
Program Flowchart	Illustrates the logical constructs included in a software program
Programming Checklist	Provides procedures, controls, and documentation list for programming maintenance

Project Cost Report Form	Displays the time each activity is projected to start and finish or has actually started or finished, its narrative description, the activity number, the budgeted cost, the actual cost, the estimated cost-to-complete, and variances
Project Plan	A group of documents detailing how a project or program will be planned, organized, and controlled, regarding topics like scheduling, quality assurance, configuration management, and so on
Project Schedule Report Form	Displays the time each activity is projected to start or stop or has actually started or stopped, its float, its narrative description, its variance, and activity number
Prototyping Checklist	Lists activities and deliverables needed for developing a model of a software product
Quality-Circles Checklist	Provides list of quality-circle opportunities
Quality-Circles Plan	Improves productivity for the company by focusing on processes, not people
Record Layout Form	Describes the characteristics of a record that makeup a particular file
Report Layout Form	Displays how reports should appear when printed on paper
Request for Proposal Plan	Procure subcontract management products and services and provide formal disciplines for the decision making process
Requirements Definition Document	Describes those capabilities, features, and other criteria that a future software system must address
Resource Histogram	Shows a profile of how one or more people are, or will be, used on a project over a period of time
Resource Usage Form	Records data on the usage of a resource employed on one or more activities
Resource Usage Report Form	Shows data on the planned, actual, and projected uses of resources assigned to a project
Risk Assessment Checklist	Lists the possible occurrences that can affect the outcome of a project
Runbook Checklist	Provides details, such as steps and their sequences, for a particular job executed on a computer

"S" Cost Curve	A cumulative curve displaying the accumulation of costs over a period of time
Scratch-Tape Reuse Form	Provides fast and efficient method of recording storage, retrieval, and distribution of scratch tapes
Software Documentation Checklist	Provides a listing of all software policies, procedures, manuals, diagrams, illustrations, and specifications required for a data processing organization, such as for a project or department
Software Ergonomics Checklist	Lists the characteristics to incorporate in software during its construction
Software Program Distribution Form	Identifies distribution, maintain control, and perform archiving
Software Program Requirement Log	Provides instructions and information when the software program is input, e.g. handling, processing, and control of requirements
Software Quality-Assurance Plan	Defines responsibilities and tasks to ensure application software agrees with project standards
Software Version Form	Reflects most current configuration of each software version
Standards and Guidelines Manual	A compilation of procedures, policies, and reference material that personnel can refer to during the development, maintenance, and operational activities of a data processing facility
Statement of Work	An agreement between the project manager and the user that defines the terms and conditions for conducting and completing a project
Statistical Quality-Control Checklist	Defines parameters and evaluation criteria for statistical control
Statistical Quality-Control Graphs	Monitor productivity and quality
Status Update Form	A mechanism for recording the status, or amount of completion, of each task in a Network Diagram or Bar Chart
Structure Chart	Illustrates the modular structure of a system, specifically software, and the relationship of those modules to one another
Structured English	Describes in a natural language method what occurs in a system

Student Handout	A document that training attendees receive and which contains copies of viewfoils and reference materials that they can use at their workstation
Subcontractor Requirements List Form	Guarantees a comprehensive, formal itemized set of end-item deliverables and provides a summary of requirements referencing specifications
Subsystem Test Report Form	Documents test results that describe tests and techniques used and compares "actuals" with "expected" outcomes
System Access Controls Checklist	Lists items to check so that no control problems exist with using the hardware or software of a computing system
System Conversion Checklist	Provides conversion preparation and activities list
System Conversion Plan	Establishes requirements, procedures, and special programming
System Incidence Log Form	Provides system incidence information, e.g. program identification and action assignments
System Performance Graph	Identifies visually how well the system is performing with respect to current benchmarks, e.g. budget, labor hours, and equipment units
System Productivity Graph	Identifies how well the system is performing with respect to current benchmarks, e.g. equipment state, tuning, and software
Systems Flowchart	Shows the manual and automated activities that occur within a system and its major components
System/Subsystem Specifications Checklist	Provides list of design, test, and performance activities
System Test Report Form	Documents test results that describe tests and techniques used
System Upgrade Checklist	Identifies whether upgrades are realistic, value-added, and cost-effective
System Utilization Log Form	Provides system utilization information, e.g. media used and change activity
Tape-Reel Archive Form	Provides fast and efficient method of recording storage, retrieval, and archiving of tape reels

Test Plan	Describes details on planning a test of a new or revised computing system along with the techniques used and the expected results of the test
Test Report Form	Describes procedures and techniques including unit tests, test drivers, and inbound and outbound inputs (when boundaries exist) to compare "actuals" with "expected" outcomes
Training Plan	Describes the extent and level of training that will occur within the next year
Training Schedule	Lists or shows when courses will occur, the resources to conduct them, the instructors with the requisite skills, and the location of the training
User Manual	Instructions, illustrations, charts, and other documentation on the use of a computer, including hardware and software
Verification/Validation Plan	Provides software verification/validation tools and techniques which increase confidence of software quality
Verification/Validation Test Checklist	Provides list of test and performance activities
Verification/Validation Test Completion Report Form	Provides baseline test completion report
Work Breakdown Structure	Shows hierarchically the tasks and subtasks in an inverted tree format to be performed on a project

REFERENCES

Awad, Elias M. *Business Data Processing*. Englewood Cliffs, NJ: Prentice Hall, 1980.

Beizer, B. *Software Testing Techniques*. New York: Van Nostrand Reinhold, 1983.

Biggs, Charles, Evan Birks, and William Atkins. *Managing the Systems Development Process*. Englewood Cliffs, NJ: Prentice Hall, 1980.

Boar, Bernard. *Application Prototyping*. New York: Wiley, 1984.

Boehm, B. W. *Software Engineering Economics*. Englewood Cliffs, NJ: Prentice Hall, 1982.

Bohl, Marilyn. *Information Processing* (4th ed.). Chicago: Science Research Associates, 1984.

Booth, G. M. *The Design of Complex Information Systems*. New York: McGraw-Hill, 1983.

Brooks, F. P. *The Mythical Man-Month*. Reading, PA: Addison-Wesley, 1975.

Capron, H. L. *Systems Analysis and Design*. Reading, PA: Benjamin/Cummings, 1986.

Capron, H. L., and Brian K. Williams. *Computers and Data Processing* (2nd ed.). Menlo Park, CA: Benjamin/Cummings, 1986.

Chandor, Anthony. *The Penguin Dictionary of Computers*. New York: Penguin Books, 1982.

Cho, Chin-Kuei. *An Introduction to Software Quality Control*. New York: Wiley, 1980.

Connell, John L., and Linda B. Shafer. *The Professional User's Guide to Acquiring Software*. New York: Van Nostrand Reinhold, 1987.

Date, C. J. *An Introduction to Database Systems*. Reading, PA: Addison-Wesley, 1986.

Davis, William S. *Computers and Business Information Processing*. Reading, PA: Addison-Wesley, 1981.

De Marco, Tom. *Controlling Software Projects: Management, Measurement, and Estimation*. Englewood Cliffs, NJ: Prentice Hall, 1982.

De Marco, Tom. *Structured Analysis and System Specification*. Englewood Cliffs, NJ: Prentice Hall, 1978.

Dickinson, Brian. *Developing Structured Systems*. New York: Yourdon Press, 1980.

Duncan, Acheson. *Quality Control and Industrial Statistics* (5th ed.). Homewood, IL: Richard D. Irwin, Inc., 1986.

Fitzgerald, Jerry. *Fundamentals of Systems Analysis*. New York: Wiley, 1987.

Galitz, Wilbert O. *Humanizing Office Automation*. Wellesley: QED Information Sciences, 1984.

Gane, Chris, and Trish Sarson. *Structured Systems Analysis: Tools and Techniques.* Englewood Cliffs, NJ: Prentice Hall, 1979.

Harper, W. L. *Data Processing Documentation: Standards, Procedures, and Applications.* Englewood Cliffs, NJ: Prentice Hall, 1980.

Hatley, Derek J., and Imtiaz A. Pirbhai. *Strategies for Real-Time System Specification.* New York: Dorset, 1987.

Hetzel, W. *The Complete Guide to Software Testing.* Wellesley, MA: QED Information Sciences, 1985.

Kapp, Dan, and Joe Leben. *IMS Programming Techniques* (2nd ed.). New York: Van Nostrand Reinhold, 1986.

Kirk, Frank G. *Total System Development for Information Systems.* New York: Wiley, 1973.

Kliem, Ralph L. *AHI'S Productivity Sourcebook.* New York: Alexander Hamilton Institute, 1988.

Kliem, Ralph L. *Developing a Cost-Effective Company Operations Manual.* New York: Alexander Hamilton Institute, 1986.

Kliem, Ralph L. *The Secrets of Successful Project Management.* New York: Wiley, 1986.

Martin, J., and C. McClure. *Software Maintenance: The Problem and Its Solution.* Englewood Cliffs, NJ: Prentice Hall, 1983.

Maynard, H. B. *Industrial Engineering Handbook* (3rd ed.). New York: McGraw-Hill, 1971.

Myers, Glenford J. *The Art of Software Testing.* New York: Wiley, 1979.

O'Brien, James A. *Computers in Business Management.* Homewood, IL: Irwin, 1982.

Page-Jones, Meilir. *The Practical Guide to Structured Systems Design.* Englewood Cliffs, NJ: Prentice Hall, 1988.

Page-Jones, Meilir. *Practical Project Management: Restoring Quality to DP Projects and Systems.* New York: Dorset, 1985.

Perry, William F. *Computer Control and Security: A Guide for Managers and Systems Analysts.* New York: Wiley, 1981.

Shelly, Gary B., and Thomas J. Cashman. *Business Systems Analysis and Design.* Fullerton, CA: Anaheim, 1978.

Shelly, Gary B. and Thomas J. Cashman, *Introduction to Flowcharting and Computer Programming Logic.* Fullerton, CA: Anaheim, 1978.

Toffler, Alvin. *The Third Wave.* New York: Morrow, 1980.

Van Duyn, J. *The DP Professional's Guide to Writing Effective Technical Communications.* New York: Wiley, 1982.

Weinberg, G. *The Psychology of Computer Programming.* New York: Van Nostrand Reinhold, 1971.

Yourdon, Edward. *Structured Design.* New York: Yourdon Press, 1978.

Index